Breakfast at O'Rourke's

BREAKFAST AT O'Rourke's

NEW CUISINE
FROM A
CLASSIC
AMERICAN
DINER

Brian O'Rourke

Wesleyan University Press | Middletown, Connecticut

Wesleyan University Press

Middletown CT 06459

www.wesleyan.edu/wespress

© 2015 Brian O'Rourke

Unless otherwise noted,

all photographs by Tom Hopkins

All rights reserved

Manufactured in the United States of America

Designed by Mindy Basinger Hill

Typeset in Calluna

Wesleyan University Press is a member of the
Green Press Initiative. The paper used
in this book meets their minimum requirement
for recycled paper.

Library of Congress Cataloging-in-Publication Data

O'Rourke, Brian, 1951–

Breakfast at O'Rourke's: new cuisine from a classic
American diner / Brian O'Rourke.

    pages   cm

Includes index.

ISBN 978-0-8195-7499-2 (pbk.: alk. paper)

1. Cooking, American. 2. O'Rourke's (Restaurant)

1. O'Rourke's (Restaurant) II. Title.

TX715.O378 2015

641.5973—dc23   2014040577

5 4 3 2 1

NOTE *I have tried to correctly scale the recipes in this book for the home cook.*
If you find any questionable quantities or instructions, please let me know at the diner,
or let Wesleyan University Press know, so that we can correct the next printing.

To Grandmother Noonie, and my many other family members and friends who have helped me in so many ways for so many years, and in memory of my friend and mentor, Dr. Bob Wolfe, whose guidance inspired the creation of this cookbook

Contents

Introduction

The year was 1959. I was eight years old and a third grader at St. John's School in Middletown, Connecticut. Little did I know that the events of that year would forever change my life.

St. John's School is located at one of the busiest intersections in Middletown—the junction of St. John's Square, Main Street, and Hartford Avenue. The school property actually sits at the base of the Arrigoni Bridge, which spans the Connecticut River and links Middletown with Portland, Connecticut. Hartford Avenue leads to Route 9, a major north-south artery that hugs the Connecticut River.

On most days my father, Bernie O'Rourke, who was the recreation director for the town of Middletown, took me to and from school. St. John's had no transportation system, and all the students were dropped off or would walk or bike to school.

Diagonally across the street from the school stood O'Rourke's Diner, which was owned by my uncle John. When he bought in 1941, it was a wooden structure. Shortly after purchasing the diner, John went off to war and served as a captain in the U.S. Army. While he was away, his wife Kathleen (my aunt Kay) assumed the responsibilities of the family business.

When John was discharged from the army, he stopped at the Mountain View Diner Company in New Jersey, which specialized in aluminum-and-steel diner facilities. He purchased a new diner to replace the wooden structure. Today Mountain View #221 still sits on the corner of Main and Hartford.

One fateful afternoon my father was delayed in coming to school, and he asked that I cross the street and wait at the diner for him. Three crossing guards at the busy intersection helped me traverse the constant stream of cars. Once I was inside the diner, Uncle John put me to work bringing up supplies from the basement storage area. I could manage everything on the supply list with the exception of the milk crates, which were too heavy. In addition, he supplied me with a broom and had me sweep the floor of the diner.

That trip across the street from school was so enjoyable that it began a lifelong affiliation with O'Rourke's Diner. From that point on I would regularly traverse the street each day to work at the diner. In the late fifties and sixties, the diner was open twenty-four hours a day and served typical diner food and a variety of specials. There was always a blue-plate special, which cost ninety-nine cents, and a less expensive menu option that cost forty-nine cents. Monday was the pork loin special; Tuesday, the daisy ham special; Wednesday, the roast beef special; Thursday, corned beef and cabbage; and Friday, seafood casserole. Less expensive blue plate specials were typical comfort foods like macaroni and cheese and meatloaf. During my elementary school years, one of the head cooks, Pat Magnano, would hide a quarter somewhere in the diner. If my cleaning expertise was worth anything, I would find the twenty-five cents, which was mine for the keeping. Besides earning twenty-five cents a day, I also had a paper route. Quite an income for someone my age!

As my elementary school years continued, I was given greater responsibility in the diner, including a wide variety of food preparation chores. I can remember peeling potatoes, almost on a daily basis. When I reached high school age, I was given my first opportunity to "work the grill." Suddenly I felt like a little man doing a big man's job. I became the grill man on the night shift like a professional short-order cook. In those days the grill was part of the counter, so food was actually cooked in the "front of the house."

In 1976 Uncle John retired, and I purchased the diner in partnership with my cousin, John Sweeney O'Rourke. During the next several years many changes

occurred in my personal life. My son, Patrick, was born. I bought a home, sold it, and bought a second home. The diner remained a twenty-four-hour operation with Cousin John and me each working a twelve-hour shift. Then, in 1985, I had the opportunity to purchase John's share of the diner. From that point on, we began to make fundamental changes in the operation of O'Rourke's. We were no longer a round-the-clock operation and were open instead just for breakfast and lunch. We continued to feature all our own homemade breads, soups, and breakfast and lunch specials, but we closed each day mid-afternoon.

Much of the inspiration for the creative success of the diner was homegrown. My maternal grandmother, Noonie, lived with us in Middletown from 1951 until the mid-1960s when I was growing up. Noonie brought her culinary talents to America from her birthplace in Sicily. Each day after school, first I did my paper route and then, when I came home from school, Noonie would have baked bread, made a homemade soup and a pasta, whether homemade ravioli, tortellini, or some other type, and, of course, there was always a pot of sauce simmering on the stove. Now, each day when I go to the diner, I think of Noonie. The smells and tastes that emanated from our house were an incredible source of inspiration for me.

In addition to what I learned at home, I had the opportunity to visit and spend time with a number of restaurateurs or bakers in the Middletown area. From them I learned the incredible craft of baking. Manny Marino owned a restaurant and bakery around the corner from the diner. I would stop in at Marino's and see Manny proofing rolls and breads.

On August 31, 2006, a fateful event occurred. Our steam cheeseburger oven was left on overnight, overheated, and caused a fire in the diner. The fire roared out of control, destroying the entire interior. The only thing that was salvaged, thanks to the heroic efforts of the local fire department, was the shell of the Mountain View #221.

A rebuilding committee, which featured a number of loyal customers, including Wesleyan University employees, was formed to rebuild the diner. On February 11, 2008, the rebuilt diner opened, to the delight of many.

Over the years the diner began to attract local, statewide, regional, and national recognition for its creative and delicious, upscale, gourmet meals. O'Rourke's Diner has been selected as "Best of Connecticut" by *Connecticut Magazine* and "Best of New England" by *Yankee Magazine*. In addition, it has been featured on the Food Network's *Diners, Drive-Ins and Dives*.

Since it is a diner, our busiest time of the day is often in the morning. The customers value our warm welcome, our homemade breads, and our extensive breakfast menu. On weekends our menu expands to include approximately sixty breakfast choices and specials. On a typical weekend day, the line of new and familiar customers extends out the door and down the sidewalk.

As O'Rourke's Diner enters its eighth decade, we take special pride in sharing with you some of our most popular breakfast recipes.

Omelets

The Dubliner Omelet

THE DUBLINER OMELET

Omelets are essentially eggs with a variety of ingredients used as fillings and/or mixed into the egg batter.

My "Dubliner" omelet (a customer favorite) is served with Irish bacon, fingerling potatoes, and Irish soda bread topped with my raspberry jam.

There are many keys to making a great omelet. If you use butter to grease your pan, you will have a good omelet, but if you use Irish butter, then you will have a better omelet. (Irish butter has a higher concentration of butter fat and can be found in most grocery stores.) The temperature of the pan makes a difference, as does the quality and temperature of your eggs. Using room temperature eggs makes for a better omelet, and I suggest letting eggs sit on the counter for about two hours before you prepare the dish. Once you master a basic omelet, you can then experiment with different ingredients and flavors. Some prefer raw ingredients in their omelet, while others like to sauté their ingredients and then add them. Condiments and sauces are also a great way to alter the appearance, and taste, of your basic omelet.

2 slices Irish bacon (see Note)

2 tablespoons vegetable shortening
or butter, divided

½ cup Corned Beef Hash (page 6)

3 medium-sized eggs

¼ cup shredded cheddar cheese

Salt and pepper to taste

Irish Soda Bread (page 77), for serving

Raspberry Jam (page 8), for serving

Cook the Irish bacon in a skillet over medium heat until golden brown. Remove the bacon and set on paper towels to drain. Pour off excess bacon fat, and melt 1 tablespoon of the shortening or butter in the skillet over low heat, then add the corned beef hash. Cook until browned, then turn off the heat.

In a bowl, whisk the eggs thoroughly. In a second skillet, melt the remaining 1 tablespoon of shortening or butter over medium heat, then pour in the eggs. When the eggs begin to cook, put the browned corned beef hash across the middle of the egg. (Envision your omelet being a trifold with your ingredients in the center.) Sprinkle on the cheddar cheese and let it melt. When the eggs are cooked but still moist, fold each edge of the omelet over the hash. Flip the omelet over, so that the seam is on the bottom. Cook 1 minute more. (Avoid overcooking—the inside should stay moist.) Top with the Irish bacon strips. Serve with fingerling potatoes and a slice or two of Irish soda bread smeared with butter and some homemade raspberry jam.

NOTE *Irish bacon is great! It is taken from the center cut of the pork loin and is more thickly sliced than regular bacon. You can find it in specialty stores, but feel free to use regular bacon if that's what you have on hand.*

Corned Beef Hash

Serves 6

When making hash, I cook the corned beef a day before grinding it in a food processor. Leaving the corned beef and potatoes in the fridge for a day makes the grinding process easier. If you would like a more "rustic" hash, hand-chop the potatoes rather than grinding them.

This hash is used as a filling for omelets or a side for any style of eggs. When it is served as a side, I put a little butter on the griddle and cook it to heat the hash through and give it a nice crispy texture. You can also add butter to a skillet and cook until both sides are brown and crisp.

2	pounds cooked corned beef
4	medium potatoes, peeled and boiled
3	medium-sized eggs
1	teaspoon celery seed
1	teaspoon Cajun seasoning
1	teaspoon dry mustard (preferably Coleman's)
½	cup ketchup
2–3	tablespoons butter, for browning hash

Finely chop the corned beef and cooked potatoes in a food processor. Pulse until the mixture is very fine but still has some texture—be careful not to make it a baby food consistency! Dump the meat and potato mixture out into a bowl and add the remaining ingredients, except the butter, and mix by hand until they all come together. It is ready to be used as a filling for omelets. To serve as a side, form the mixture into patties 3 inches in diameter. Melt the butter in a skillet over low heat, then brown the patties on both sides.

Cajun Fingerlings

The price of fingerling potatoes when compared with regular is a bit more, but the flavor is in another world. I absolutely love marble-size fingerlings for my dishes. At the diner, we prepare about twenty pounds of potatoes at a time. Inevitably, they will not all be the same size, which makes it more difficult to have a consistent cooking time. I strongly recommend choosing potatoes similar in size when going to the market for your own cooking, so that all your potatoes are done cooking around the same time.

We serve fingerlings with our Eggs Oscar (one of our many takes on the traditional Eggs Benedict), as well as the Dubliner Omelet (a customer favorite). For lunch, I create an appetizer by adding chopped bacon to a bowl of fingerling potatoes, topping them with shredded cheddar cheese, and finishing them off by roasting them in the oven. Recently, I served fingerlings as a side with steak and mushrooms. They also make a great potato salad, and can even be grated raw over a green salad. The possibilities are endless.

2   pounds fingerling potatoes

2   tablespoons salt

2   tablespoons vegetable shortening
    or bacon fat

1   onion, diced

    Cajun seasoning to taste

Rinse the potatoes and place them in a pot of cold water. Be sure there is enough water to cover potatoes. Add the salt and bring the water to a boil; continue boiling for 2 minutes and then turn off the heat. Leave the potatoes in the pan, checking them with a fork every 2 to 3 minutes until cooked. If you have potatoes of different sizes, remove the smaller potatoes as they are done. Drain the potatoes and slice the larger ones in half.

Melt the shortening or bacon fat in a skillet, then add the onions and potatoes. When the potatoes have browned, toss with the Cajun seasoning, and enjoy!

Raspberry Jam

Variations to this recipe can be found on the Certo fruit pectin package. I suggest following the directions exactly the first time you prepare this recipe. After that, feel free to experiment with seasonal fruits. At the diner, I really do a lot of mixing and matching or, as I like to call it, "making the leprechauns dance!" My favorite raspberries to use are yellow raspberries. At one point, I had a local farmer, Ed Farrington, put in 100 yards of yellow raspberries just for the diner.

What is the difference between jam and jelly? Jelly wiggles, while jam sits. A jam or preserve is cooked down; it consists of more fruit and less sugar. Because of the higher fruit content, jam is typically more expensive than jelly.

4	cups frozen raspberries (or fresh, if in season)
2	cups sugar
2	apples, cored and quartered
1	orange, peeled and quartered
3	cinnamon sticks
1	pouch liquid fruit pectin (I use Certo brand)

Put all the ingredients into a large saucepan and bring to a simmer over low heat. Continue to simmer for approximately 40 minutes. Let cool and store in glass jars in the refrigerator. You can store jam for about 4 weeks in the refrigerator. At the diner, we refrigerate our preserves in quart-size containers because of the volume we use daily. However, you could can or freeze the jam, if you prefer.

OMELETS

The Bob Wolfe Omelet

MENU

- The Bob Wolfe Omelet
- Red Flannel Hash
- Home Fries
- Irish Brown Bread "Scones"

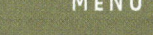

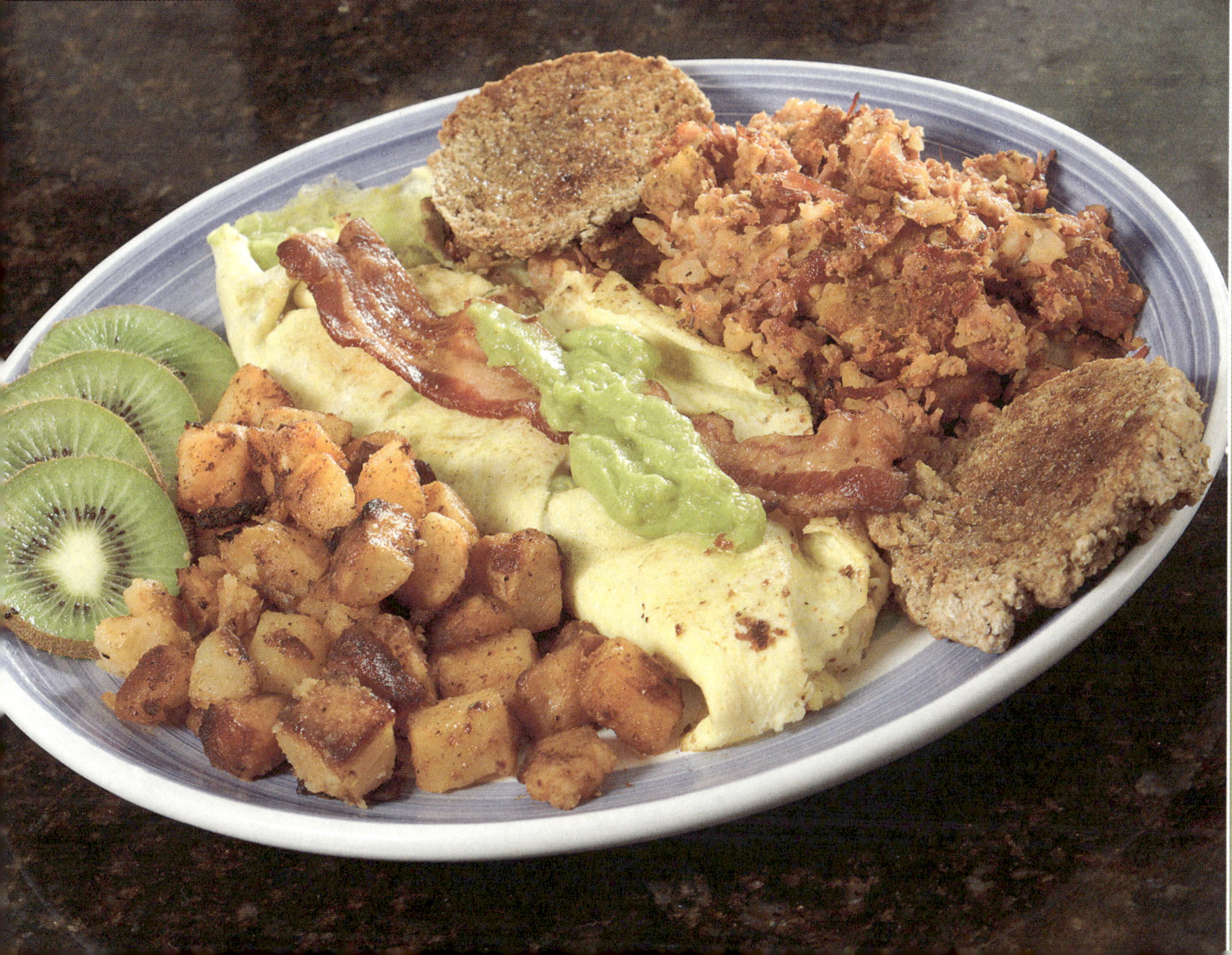

THE BOB WOLFE OMELET

I met Bob Wolfe more than two decades ago. Bob had just been named principal of Korn Elementary School in Durham, Connecticut. I lived about a mile from the school. The then–superintendent of schools Dr. William Breck came to the diner and introduced me to Bob. It was the beginning of an incredible friendship. I shared with Bob that I had always wanted to work with children. From that day on, I spent a part of each Wednesday at his school, teaching life skills to an academically challenged student. That expanded to helping his food service ladies, working in a summer camp, supporting fund-raisers, and teaching adult education cooking classes. Bob was on the committee to rebuild the diner after the 2006 fire and was instrumental in ensuring that the diner opened again. This omelet started as his special order, and then it was then placed on the menu. Today it is the second-best-seller after the Dubliner. Like our friendship, the omelet is special.

2	slices bacon
2–4	tablespoons chopped tomatoes
3	medium-sized eggs
2	tablespoons butter
2	slices provolone cheese
2–4	tablespoons Guacamole (page 14)
2–4	tablespoons Red Flannel Hash (page 83)
	Fresh fruit of your choice, for garnish

In a skillet over medium heat, cook the bacon until crispy. Put it on paper towels to drain, then crumble. Pour off most of the bacon fat, reserving about two tablespoons in the skillet. Sauté tomatoes in the fat over low heat until just cooked.

In a bowl, whisk the eggs thoroughly. In a skillet, melt the butter over medium heat and pour in the eggs. When the eggs begin to cook, lay the provolone, bacon, tomatoes, Guacamole, and hash across the middle of the omelet. (Envision your omelet being a trifold with your ingredients in the center.) When the eggs are cooked, fold each edge of the omelet over the hash. Flip the omelet over, so that the seam is on the bottom. Cook 1 minute more. (Avoid overcooking—the inside should stay moist.) Garnish with fruit.

Home Fries

There are so many variables at play when you are making home fries. Even at the diner, where we follow the same recipe and have made them a million times, they don't always turn out the same. The outcome with home fries depends on the quality of the potatoes, the size of the potato when diced, boiling the potatoes to the proper texture, frying them with the right amount of onion and spices, and how busy it is at the diner.

6 medium potatoes, any variety, cut into ¾-inch dice, peeled or not

1 stick margarine or butter

1 onion, diced

3 tablespoons paprika

1 teaspoon salt, plus more for the potato-boiling water

1 teaspoon black pepper

1 teaspoon garlic powder

In a large pot, cover the diced potatoes with cold salted water. Bring them water to a boil, then turn off the heat and check the potatoes for doneness every 2 minutes; when a fork can easily be inserted and removed, they are done. Rinse and shock the cooked potatoes in cold water. Drain well.

NOTE *Although it's not necessary, I refrigerate my cooked potatoes overnight and grill them the next morning. I like the consistency that results with this method.*

Melt the margarine or butter in a large skillet over medium heat. Add the potatoes, onion, spices, and salt. Cook until the Home Fries have a nice brown color.

IRISH BROWN BREAD "SCONES"

Irish Brown Bread can be found throughout Ireland, and everyone's grandmother makes the best, according to the family. There are countless variations of brown bread. Once you have perfected the basic recipe, explore different flavors and textures by experimenting with various grains and add-ins. You can also try different shapes by using a muffin pan or making round loaves. Be sure to adjust cooking times accordingly.

Our Irish Brown Bread was once served at the White House as part of a program to feed the hungry. What a thrill I had when the FedEx truck arrived at the diner to pick up my bread for delivery to 1600 Pennsylvania Avenue!

2	cups whole wheat flour	½	teaspoon baking powder
1¼	cups all-purpose flour	½	teaspoon salt
1	cup wheat bran (crumbled bran flakes or All-Bran may be substituted)	½	stick butter, plus more for greasing the cookie sheet
¼	cup sugar	2	cups buttermilk
1	teaspoon baking soda		

Preheat the oven to 350°F and grease a cookie sheet.

Mix all the dry ingredients together into a bowl. Cut in the butter using a paddle blade on a stand mixer, or hand-cut into the dry ingredients using a pastry blender or your fingertips. Add the buttermilk and stir just until incorporated. Do not overmix! Using a large ice cream scoop (#20, which holds about 2 ounces), place the dough on the prepared cookie sheet about 4 inches apart. Place in the oven as quickly as possible from the time the mixture is incorporated!

Bake for 12 minutes. Rotate the cookie sheet in the oven and bake for about 5 more minutes or until the brown bread feels solid to the touch. Remove from the oven, let sit for 10 minutes, then cool on a wire rack. The scones may be split in half horizontally and grilled with butter.

Variation GUINNESS-OATMEAL BROWN BREAD

To make, substitute 1 cup of Guinness stout for 1 cup of buttermilk and 1 cup of old-fashioned rolled oats for ½ cup of all-purpose flour and ½ cup of whole wheat flour.

Add 1 cup of raisins or ½ cup of sunflower seeds if desired.

GUACAMOLE

Guacamole goes with so many things—eggs, chicken, seafood. You name it. Guacamole and tomato makes a great summer sandwich, as does guacamole and cucumber.

4	ripe avocados
¼	cup diced red onion
¼	cup diced fresh tomato
¼	cup minced onion
¼	cup fresh cilantro leaves cut into chiffonade (see Note)
	Juice of 2 limes
1	teaspoon chili powder
1	teaspoon kosher salt
1	teaspoon cumin seeds, toasted

Cut the avocados in half and remove the pits. Using a spoon, scoop out the avocado flesh into a medium bowl. Mash avocados and then stir in the additional ingredients. Let sit overnight, covered tightly, to allow the flavors to blend. (If the Guacamole is not tightly covered, the avocados will oxidize and turn brown overnight.)

NOTE *Chiffonade refers to herbs or leafy vegetables cut into thin strips or ribbons. To make anything into chiffonade, stack the leaves, roll them up tightly like a cigar, and cut them crosswise into very thin strips.*

Tri-Pesto Omelet

TRI-PESTO OMELET

When I first started experimenting with pesto, I made a roasted red pepper pesto with my neighbor's ripe bell peppers. There is nothing like using fresh ingredients for a pesto! If you like a little spice, try adding some poblano peppers to the mixture.

This particular omelet started with a basic omelet filled with roasted red pepper pesto. Eventually, I got a little inspiration from the leprechauns and decided to add my spinach pesto. Eventually, I mastered a caramelized onion pesto, and the tri-pesto omelet was created!

3 medium-sized eggs

2 tablespoons butter

1 tablespoon Onion Pesto (page 20)

1 tablespoon Spinach Pesto (page 20)

1 tablespoon Roasted Red Pepper Pesto (page 20)

¼ cup store-bought or homemade ricotta cheese (page 71)

A small amount of each pesto, for garnish

In a bowl, whisk the eggs thoroughly. Melt the butter in a skillet over medium heat, and pour in the eggs. When the eggs begin to cook, spread the three pestos across the middle of the egg, one next to the other. (Envision your omelet being a trifold with your ingredients in the center.) Spoon the ricotta across the top of the pestos. When the eggs are cooked, fold over each edge of the omelet over the pestos. Flip the omelet over, so that the seam is on the bottom. Cook 1 minute more. (Avoid overcooking—the inside should stay moist.) Use the remaining pesto to garnish the top of the omelet. Drawing the Italian flag would not be inappropriate! Serve with Colcannon and Portuguese Sweet Bread. (Home Fries, page 11, are also shown in the breakfast photograph on the preceding page.)

When scrambling, frying, or poaching eggs, the size of the egg is not important. I've found that medium-sized eggs seem to give the best flavor, and so that is the size I use.

COLCANNON

One day at the diner, a customer wrote down song lyrics for me from Mary Black's song, "Colcannon." I still have these lyrics:

Did you ever eat Colcannon, made from lovely pickled cream?

With the greens and scallions mingled like a picture in a dream.

Did you ever make a hole on top to hold the melting flake

Of the creamy, flavoured butter that your mother used to make?

On chilly nights in Ireland, families would make this as a treat and serve it warm. They would always make sure to have enough to reheat for the next morning's breakfast.

The way Colcannon is prepared varies from town to town in Ireland. It is similar to how families prepare mashed potatoes here in the United States. Everyone makes it a little different by adding milk, cream, butter, and spices.

For numerous pairings, I use Colcannon as my starch. It works great with fish, especially as a base for scallops. It is a side dish for several items found on the O'Rourke's Diner menu.

6 medium potatoes, peeled and quartered— any variety will do	1 teaspoon toasted caraway seeds (see Note on next page)
1 cup minced or diced green cabbage	Salt and pepper to taste
½ stick butter, divided	

Boil the potatoes for 20 minutes or until cooked. Drain the potatoes well, and mash them. Melt 2 tablespoons of the butter in a skillet and sauté the cabbage until it softens. In a large bowl, mix together the mashed potatoes, cooked cabbage, and toasted caraway seeds until combined. Season with salt and pepper. Place in the refrigerator to cool (best if cooled overnight).

Melt the remaining 2 tablespoons of butter in skillet over medium heat. Place scoops of colcannon in the skillet, flatten somewhat, and cook the colcannon patties on both sides until a nice golden-brown crust forms. Serve warm.

NOTE *For this recipe, I toast caraway seeds. This process helps extract the oils and intensifies the flavor of the seed.*

PORTUGUESE SWEET BREAD

In the 1970s, I took a trip to Cape Cod. One early morning, around 4:00 a.m. or so, I smelled bread whose scent outweighed the salty air. I followed the scent all the way to a bakery. For the next three days, I woke up at 4:00 a.m., walked to the bakery, and learned how to make the sweet-smelling bread myself. Today, I use this bread as our house white bread. It is delicious fresh out of the oven and topped with butter.

1	cup warm water (below 115°F)
¼	cup sugar
2	tablespoons active dry yeast
½	stick butter
3	medium-sized eggs
1	cup milk, scalded
4	cups all-purpose flour

Preheat the oven to 350°F and grease 2 (9-by-5-inch) loaf pans.

In a large bowl, combine the warm water and sugar, then sprinkle the yeast over top. Set aside for about 10 minutes until the yeast activates and starts to get foamy. In another mixing bowl, combine the remaining ingredients and add to the yeast mixture. Knead the dough for about ten minutes. Form two loaves and place in the greased loaf pans. Bake for 22 minutes, then lower the oven temperature to 325°F and bake for 22 minutes more, or until the bread is golden brown and sounds hollow when you tap the top.

NOTE *Do not add any liquid over 115°F to your yeast, or it will kill your yeast and the dough will not rise.*

PESTO

Most know the name, the look, and the taste of pesto—but what is it really? The word itself originated from the Genoese pesta, *meaning "to pound and/or crush with marble and wooden pestle," which was the original method of preparation. Traditionally, pesto consists of crushed garlic, basil, and pine nuts blended with extra-virgin olive oil and Parmesan and Pecorino cheeses.*

Here at the diner I have three types of pesto on the menu: Spinach, Onion, and Roasted Red Pepper. The reason for our varieties? For starters, basil was unavailable or very pricey during the winter season; thus I used spinach instead. Pine nuts and extra-virgin olive oil also become costly on a larger scale, so I put my own twist on our three different kinds. Besides, I love the taste!

Pesto can be put in oiled ice cube trays and frozen. Remove and store in the freezer in plastic bags.

1	cup walnuts
4	cups fresh spinach leaves (for Spinach Pesto)
2	cups carmelized onions (for Onion Pesto)
2	cups roasted red bell peppers, drained (for Roasted Red Pepper Pesto)
5	cloves garlic, chopped
¾	cup olive oil
1	cup grated Parmesan cheese
	Pinch of salt
	Freshly ground black pepper to taste

Chop/pulse the walnuts a few times in a food processor, then add your main ingredient—spinach, onions, or red peppers—to the food processor and pulse again. Add the garlic and pulse a few times more. Slowly add the olive oil while the food processor is running. Pause and scrape down the sides of the food processor with a rubber spatula. Add the grated cheese and pulse again until blended. Add the salt and black pepper and pulse once more to combine.

Use as an omelet filling or serve over pasta with fresh bread.

Firecracker Omelet

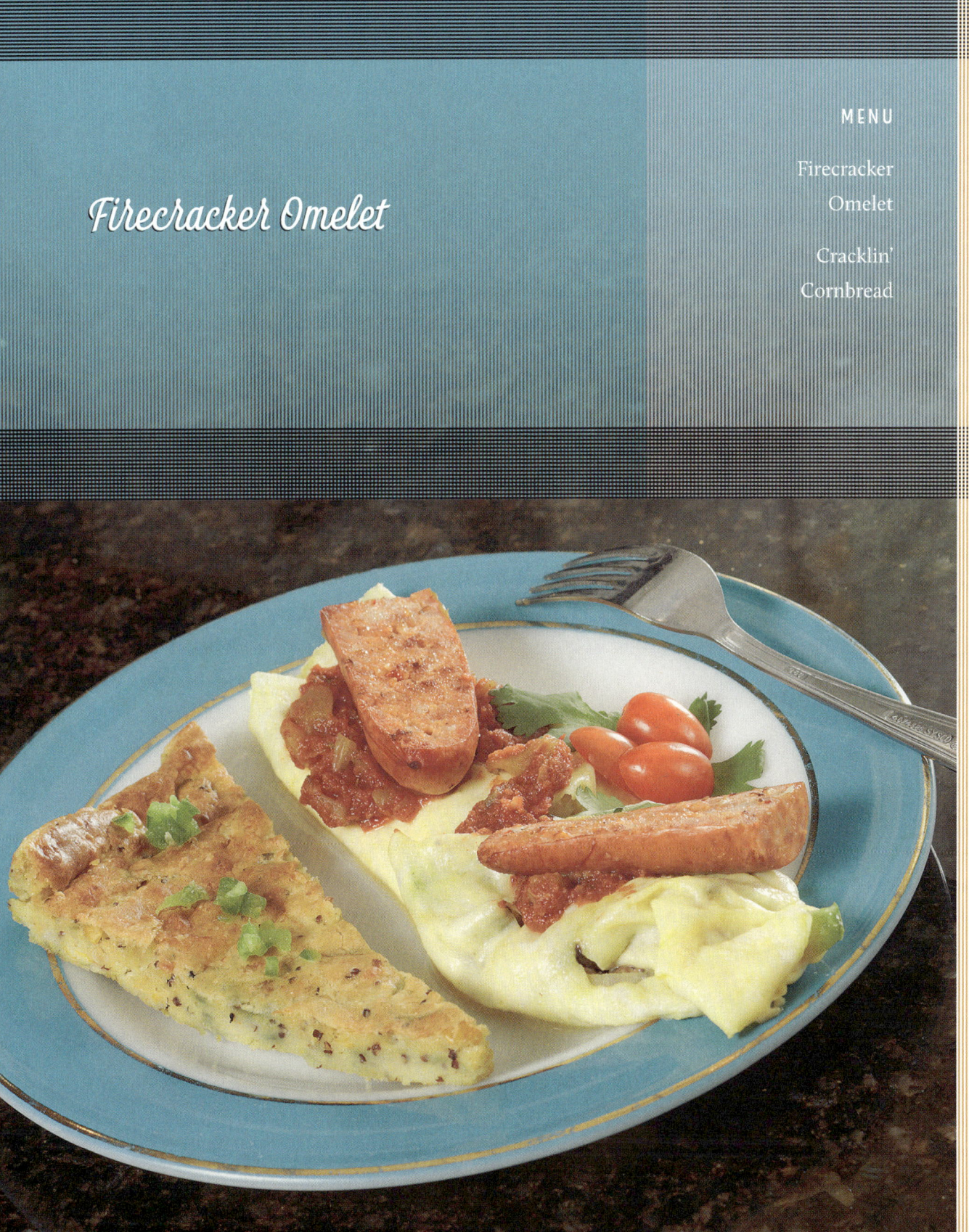

FIRECRACKER OMELET

This omelet gets much of its flavor from the onions and mushrooms, as well as a quality aged cheddar cheese. Sharp cheddar can, however, be substituted for aged cheddar cheese. The spicy kick comes from our house-made Creole Sauce, and the andouille sausage on top. Not boring, for sure!

2	slices andouille sausage (see Note)
¼	cup sliced mushrooms
¼	cup diced onions
3	medium-sized eggs
2	tablespoons vegetable shortening or butter
¼	cup shredded aged cheddar cheese
2	tablespoons Creole Sauce (page 25)
	Salt and pepper to taste

Brown the sausage in a skillet over medium heat; remove to a plate. Sauté the mushrooms and onions in the sausage grease until thoroughly cooked and slightly browned. In a medium-sized bowl, whisk the eggs thoroughly. In a second skillet, melt the shortening or butter over medium heat and pour in the whisked eggs.

When the eggs begin to cook, put the grated cheddar cheese in the middle of the egg, letting the cheese melt. (Envision your omelet being a trifold with your ingredients in the center.) Add the sautéed vegetables and Creole Sauce to the center. When the eggs are cooked, fold over each edge of the omelet. Flip the omelet over, so that the seam is on the bottom. Cook 1 minute more. (Avoid overcooking—the inside should stay juicy.) Top with the sausage.

NOTE *Lots of our sausages and other meats come from Nodine's Smokehouse, a terrific little spot in Goshen, Connecticut. You can order directly from them by visiting their website: www.nodinesmokehouse.com.*

CRACKLING CORNBREAD

This is my variation on a traditional cornbread. My cracklings are made from the fat and trimmings of corned beef, in keeping with O'Rourke's Diner's Irish-American roots. A slice of this bread holds together without crumbling and provides a rich counterpoint to our Firecracker Omelet (page 22), as well as gumbo and chili dishes. In my cornbread, I use all the listed "goodies" but you can use as many of them as you desire.

GOODIES (*your choice*)

½ cup red bell peppers, diced small

½ cup onion, diced small

1 jalapeño pepper, seeded and diced fine

2 tablespoons bacon fat or vegetable oil, plus extra for greasing the loaf pans

1 cup corn kernels, drained

1½ cups shredded aged cheddar cheese

1 cup corned beef cracklings, diced small (You make cracklings by deep-frying corned beef trimmings or bacon until very crisp and brown.)

salt and pepper to taste

DRY

2 cups all-purpose flour

2 cups cornmeal

1 tablespoon baking powder

1 teaspoon baking soda

1 teaspoon salt

1 teaspoon Cajun seasoning

WET

2 cups sour cream

¾ cup buttermilk

6 medium-sized eggs

¼ cup sugar

Preheat the oven to 350°F. Grease two (9-by-5-inch) loaf pans. (Cast iron is my preference.)

Prepare the goodies: If you're using bell pepper, onion, and/or jalapeño pepper, sauté them in the bacon fat or oil in a skillet over medium heat until slightly browned. Add the corn (if desired) and season with salt and pepper. Cook until the kernels are golden brown. Allow to cool.

Sift together all the dry ingredients in a large mixing bowl. Make a well in the middle of the mound of ingredients. Whisk together all the wet ingredients (also the sugar—it's not wet at first, but it will be when it dissolves!) in a separate bowl. Pour the wet ingredients into the well and mix, using a rubber spatula, until just blended. Don't overmix, as this can result in a tough cornbread. Fold the "goodies" into the batter until they are evenly distributed.

Pour the batter evenly into the greased loaf pans. Transfer to the oven and bake for 12 minutes, then lower the temperature to 325°F and continue baking the loaves until firm and a toothpick or paring knife inserted into the center comes out clean, approximately 20 more minutes. Allow to cool, and cut into slices for serving.

NOTE *This recipe can also be baked in a well-greased, 12-inch cast iron skillet and cut into wedges (as pictured).*

CREOLE SAUCE

Creole sauce is also known as southern marinara, sauce piquante, red gravy, and Lafayette stew. At the diner, I use a European-influenced Creole sauce rather than an Acadian-influenced Cajun sauce (although it includes Cajun seasoning!). Creole is a great sauce for an omelet with cheese, as well as a topping for chicken or catfish dishes. This sauce freezes well, allowing for advance preparation.

2	tablespoons vegetable oil
½	cup diced celery
½	cup diced onion
½	cup diced green bell pepper
2–3	cloves garlic, minced
2	(28-ounce) cans crushed tomatoes (do not drain!)
¼	cup red wine
2	bay leaves
1	tablespoon Cajun seasoning

Heat the oil in a medium saucepan over medium heat, and sauté the "trinity" of celery, onions, and peppers. When these are almost softened, add the garlic and cook for 1 minute, stirring. Add the tomatoes and simmer for an additional 5 minutes. Add the remaining ingredients and simmer until the desired consistency is acquired.

NOTE *For a thicker sauce, cook long and slow. You may also combine 2 tablespoons of cornstarch with 2 tablespoons of cold water and add a little of this mixture at a time, stirring often.*

MENU

Swiss, Crab, and
Asparagus Omelet
with Hollandaise Sauce

Pan-Fried Turnip Cakes

Nice Spice Scones

Swiss, Crab, and Asparagus Omelet

Swiss, Crab, and Asparagus Omelet
with Hollandaise Sauce

This omelet is elegant and classy. As in all our dishes, the quality of ingredients is of supreme importance. Don't skimp! Use the best, freshest crabmeat, when in season, and fresh garden asparagus. You'll thank me! Do as we do, and make this only in the spring when asparagus is best.

Originally, when I first offered this omelet at the diner, I liked to use blue crabs that were caught right at the beach. Today I purchase crab by the case, an indication that this popular omelet is definitely a keeper! (In the photo opposite, the sides differ from the recipes offered here. There is always something unexpected at O'Rourke's!)

4   stalks asparagus, trimmed

2   ounces cooked lump crabmeat, picked over for shells and cartilage

3   medium-sized eggs

1   tablespoon butter

¼   cup shredded Swiss cheese

    Salt and pepper to taste

1   tablespoon Hollandaise Sauce (page 28)

    Crumbled cooked bacon, for garnish (optional)

Blanch the asparagus briefly in salted boiling water. Shock in ice water until cooled; drain. If your crabmeat is canned, drain well.

In a bowl, whisk the eggs thoroughly. In a medium-sized skillet, melt the butter over medium heat and pour in the eggs. As the eggs begin to cook, sprinkle the shredded cheese on top of the cooking omelet. Then sprinkle the crabmeat evenly over the cheese and add the asparagus. Arrange the spears so that the attractive pointy ends protrude from both ends of the omelet. When the eggs are cooked, fold over each edge of the omelet. Flip the omelet over, so that the seam is on the bottom. Cook 1 minute more. (Avoid overcooking—the inside should stay moist.) Top with Hollandaise Sauce and sprinkle with some bacon bits (if desired) for some added color and flavor.

HOLLANDAISE SAUCE

Even some of our schooled chefs have difficulty with this sauce, so don't get discouraged! For a number of reasons, Hollandaise Sauce may break, meaning it curdles. It can break if it is too hot, too cold, too acidic (or not acidic enough), or if it cooks too long (or not long enough). If your sauce curdles, you can pulse it in a blender to smooth it out. When made properly, it can be described as an egg-bused mayonnaise. We use it for our Eggs Benedict, and as a topping for some of our omelets.

Because the Hollandaise Sauce can be difficult to make, it can be replaced with a store-bought mix that just requires adding water. Mornay Sauce can also be used as a substitute.

Since I try to avoid waste, I often use the egg whites from this recipe in an omelet, or incorporate them into bread.

2	medium-sized egg yolks	Pinch of salt
1	stick butter	Splash of hot sauce
	Juice of ½ lemon	

On the stovetop, place a *metal* mixing bowl on top of a pan of simmering water, or use a double boiler. The bottom of the bowl should be above the level of the simmering water.

Clarify the butter by putting it in the mixing bowl and allowing it to melt and eventually separate (about 25 to 30 minutes). Carefully pour the clarified butter from the bowl into a liquid measuring cup with a spout, leaving the solid milk deposits at the bottom of the bowl. Discard the solid milk deposits and wipe out the bowl.

Add the egg yolks to the mixing bowl over the pan of simmering water. (Do not allow the eggs to cook! They will if they get too hot.) Gently heat and continue to whisk the egg yolks. Slowly add the clarified butter in a steady stream, while continuing to whisk. Once the butter is incorporated, whisk in the lemon juice, salt, and hot sauce.

Pan-Fried Turnip Cakes

Turnips are from the Brassica family. When buying, I suggest visiting a local farm to ensure freshness. At the diner, I get my turnips from Preli Farm in Glastonbury, Connecticut. If a turnip is fresh, you should be able to peel and eat it just as you would an apple. I think the best turnips are purple-top turnips with a healthy green top and smooth skin.

There are several ways to prepare turnips: boiled, mashed, fried, roasted, as chips, and so on. In addition to the method described in this recipe, I like to cube and boil turnips in sugar water, just as you would with corn. Turnips can be stored approximately three weeks in the refrigerator, until you are ready to use them.

4–6 purple-top turnips, approximately 1½ pounds

1 cup old-fashioned rolled oats

½ cup honey

2 tablespoons vegetable shortening, butter, olive oil, or any fat of your choice, for frying

Salt and pepper to taste

Peel and quarter the turnips. Place in salted cold water and bring to a boil. Continue to boil until the turnips are tender, approximately 30 minutes. Drain and mash with oats and honey. Season with salt and pepper. Form into six patties (add more oatmeal, if necessary, to help bind them). Heat the shortening in skillet over medium heat. Brown the cakes on both sides in the skillet, about 3-4 minutes on each side.

NOTE *These Turnip Cakes didn't make it onto the plate in the picture, but like the Nice Spice Scones, they are a favorite at the diner and go well with many main dishes.*

NICE SPICE SCONES

In Ireland, a scone is more than just something to feed the body. It's a social event.
—*Brian O'Rourke*

The soft batter for these muffin-shaped scones can also be dropped with a scoop in soft balls, lightly floured, and patted into a low mound to bake.

Brewed Irish breakfast tea

1 cup raisins

1 ounce Irish whiskey

3 cups all-purpose flour

½ cup sugar

½ teaspoon Nice Spice (page 32)

½ teaspoon baking powder

½ stick Irish butter, plus more for greasing the pan and for serving

2 cups buttermilk

The night before: Make a pot of Irish breakfast tea. Add raisins and Irish whiskey and let soak overnight.

Preheat the oven to 375°F and grease a 12-cup muffin pan. Drain the raisins (see Note). Mix the flour, sugar, spice, and baking powder in a bowl.

Using a pastry blender or your fingertips, cut in the butter and mix until you achieve a barley-like consistency. Stir the tea-and-whiskey-soaked raisins into the dry mix. Pour the buttermilk into the center of the bowl and mix until just blended. Take care not to overmix!

Scoop the batter into the muffin cups, filling them about three-quarters full. Bake for 12 to 16 minutes, or until a toothpick inserted in the center of each comes out clean and the tops are slightly browned. Remove from the oven and immediately top with Irish butter. Let the scones sit in the tin for 5 minutes, then remove them from the tin and let them continue cooling on cooling racks. Then, as James Joyce said, "Watch the butter cry!"

Wrapped in plastic, the scones can be stored for 2 weeks. They could also be frozen.

NOTE *You can either drink the tea or freeze it in ice-cube trays to make very interesting ice cubes.*

At the diner, I use this as my spice of choice. It has a little bit of everything, so that each recipe gets a taste of everyone's favorite spices! I sometimes add a bit of dried and crumbled lavender or rose petals to this also.

3	tablespoons ground cinnamon
1	tablespoon ground ginger
1½	teaspoons ground cloves
1½	teaspoons ground allspice
1½	teaspoons ground cardamom
1½	teaspoons ground nutmeg
6	tablespoons sugar

Combine all the ingredients in a bowl. Shake together and store in an air-tight container, such as a small canning jar. It can last a year, or however long you keep your spices at home.

Other Eggs

Eggs O' Rourke

EGGS O'ROURKE

This diner favorite combines the two most popular breakfast meats with soft-scrambled eggs and Mornay Sauce for a meal of porky, cheesy goodness! Feel free to put some orange slices or a strawberry next to the fried potatoes. It does make the plate pretty, if not any closer to diet fare!

1   tablespoon Mornay Sauce (page 39)

2   slices bacon, diced

1   link breakfast sausage, diced, or 1 thin slice breakfast sausage

2   medium-sized eggs

Paprika, for garnish

Fresh fruit, for garnish

Heat and whisk the Mornay Sauce in a saucepan over medium-low heat until the sauce is hot and smooth.

Cook the bacon and sausage in a nonstick pan on medium heat until the bacon is crispy and the sausage is nicely browned (if using the loose breakfast sausage, break it up with a spatula). In a small bowl, beat the eggs with a fork, then add to the pan with the meat. Use a heat-resistant spatula or a wooden spoon to stir the mixture slowly, until the eggs are barely set and still moist. Plate the eggs and top with the Mornay Sauce; then sprinkle with paprika and add fruit. (Shown here with Portuguese Sweet Bread, page 19.)

POTATO LASAGNA

Of course we make our lasagna with potatoes! What do you expect? Noodles? To let the flavors of potato and cheese shine, our version does not use tomatoes or red sauce.

The first time I tried my hand at this, it was a Picasso (a one-of-a-kind recipe that you won't find in other cookbooks), and truly an O'Rourke original. My Sicilian grandmother, "Noonie," cooked potatoes a lot, but she made her lasagna the traditional way, with noodles. Lasagna was a constant at our house, and it was always a holiday feature (my sister Maureen still makes it for Easter and Christmas). My Potato Lasagna, which is Sicilian meets Irish, is the perfect symbol of my Irish-Sicilian heritage.

This version is the original. It has seen many adaptations, but it is still a "wow." Since first making this recipe, I have used eight different potatoes (including sweet potato and turnip) and eight different cheeses. I suggest slicing potatoes on a meat slicer, if possible, to get pieces as thin as can be. Layer by layer, you can create your own masterpiece.

Potato Lasagna has become a staple for many of the diner's catered events. A recent version, called June's Garden Treat, featured turnips, broccoli, homemade ricotta, greens, zucchini, and two kinds of potatoes.

FOR THE LAYERS

Nonstick cooking spray or vegetable shortening, for the pan

3 pounds potatoes, any kind, sliced ⅛-inch thick or thinner (use a mandolin slicer or the slicing blade of your food processor)

Salt and pepper

⅓ cup grated Parmesan cheese

4 cups baby spinach, loosely packed

3 cups shredded cheese (a blend of cheddar and Swiss works perfectly)

FOR THE TOPPING

1½ cups seasoned bread crumbs

½ cup grated Parmesan cheese

2 tablespoons butter, melted

1 tablespoon Smoked Horseradish Sauce
(page 41)

Preheat the oven to 350°F. Coat a 9-by-13-inch baking dish with nonstick cooking spray, or grease with a bit of shortening.

Create the layers:

Layer 1: Cover the bottom of the baking dish with a single layer of potatoes, overlapping them. Sprinkle the potato layer with salt and pepper.

Layer 2: Sprinkle the potatoes with some of the Parmesan cheese.

Layer 3: Place about a third of the baby spinach in a layer covering the potatoes and Parmesan.

Layer 4: Sprinkle 1 cup of the cheddar and Swiss cheese mixture over the spinach.

Repeat the layers twice more, then finish with a final layer of potatoes.

Add the topping: In a small bowl, mix together the bread crumbs, the ½ cup of Parmesan cheese, and the melted butter, then spread over the top of the last layer.

Seal the top of the pan with plastic wrap and a layer of aluminum foil. The plastic wrap keeps the moisture in place, and the tin foil distributes the heat evenly. The plastic wrap should just cover the top of the dish and the foil should completely seal the plastic wrap in place. Bake until the potatoes are tender, about 90 minutes. Remove the foil and plastic wrap and allow the topping to brown. Cool somewhat before slicing. Top with Smoked Horseradish Sauce.

This dish is even better the next day!

MORNAY SAUCE

To make this sauce, I start with a béchamel, one of the "mother sauces." Once this cream sauce has been created, I add cheese to get a Mornay. At the diner, Mornay Sauce is used as a topping for some of our variations on the classic Eggs Benedict, as well as a few of our scrambled egg dishes. Eggs O'Rourke calls for only a small amount of this sauce, but you will find Mornay Sauce terrific for many other dishes, including as a base for pasta primavera and macaroni and cheese, and it's great over chicken, scallops, and baked potatoes.

1	tablespoon olive oil		2	tablespoons all-purpose flour
¼	cup finely chopped onion		¼	cup shredded cheddar cheese and Swiss cheese, mixed
1	clove garlic, minced			Salt to taste
1	bay leaf			White pepper to taste
2	cups half-and-half			Nutmeg to taste
2	tablespoons butter			

Heat the oil in a medium saucepan over medium heat. Add the onion and garlic, and sauté until translucent. Add the bay leaf and half-and-half and cook for 10 minutes.

In a separate saucepan, melt the butter over medium heat. Sprinkle in the flour, while whisking constantly, to make a blond roux (see Note). Add the roux and the cheddar and Swiss cheeses to the half-and-half sauce, and stir until the cheese is melted. Add the salt, white pepper, and nutmeg. Continue to cook over low heat until the sauce is thickened, about 15 minutes.

NOTE *A roux (pronounced "roo") is a base of flour and fat used to thicken and flavor many Creole and Cajun dishes, as well as soups and sauces. It is fairly easy to make; however, it is important to stir the mixture constantly until it reaches the desired color, which may take from 3 to 15 minutes, depending on the color desired (blond, brown, or dark)—the darker the roux, the stronger the flavor. As a roux continues to darken, it loses some of its thickening power and takes on a nuttier flavor. Once you have the color you want, remove the pan from the heat and continue stirring until it has cooled down a bit and there's no risk of burning. If black specks appear in your roux, then it has burned and you must start over.*

Smoked Horseradish Sauce

My ideal salad would have romaine hearts, Smoked Horseradish Sauce, crushed cashews, and Parmesan cheese. I am grateful this sauce is not in-house at all times because I would definitely get caught eating it all.

This sauce is extremely versatile. Smoked Horseradish Sauce can be used instead of Hollandaise Sauce on any Eggs Benedict recipe for a completely different flavor combination. The other night, I topped a zucchini walnut cake with a drop of smoked horseradish, and it added an entirely new dimension. We top our Polish omelet with this sauce; it's a great complement to the kielbasa and Swiss cheese. Pairing it with onion rings takes a simple appetizer to a whole different level. Try it on a traditional Reuben with a little mustard in place of Thousand Island dressing, and you will be delighted!

1½ cups mayonnaise

½ cup prepared horseradish

1½ teaspoons Worcestershire sauce

¼ teaspoon liquid smoke
(go light—it's powerful stuff!)

Whisk together all the ingredients until thoroughly blended.

NOTE *This sauce can easily be refrigerated for a month or more.*

Eggs Oscar

EGGS OSCAR

This favorite is derived from the classic Steak Oscar, where a filet mignon is topped with crabmeat, asparagus, and Béarnaise sauce. Here we've swapped out the crab for shrimp and the Béarnaise for Hollandaise. This rich and decadent twist on Eggs Benedict can be brought to your home table for much less bother than you would think!

2 tablespoons Hollandaise Sauce (page 28)	2 medium-sized eggs
1 English muffin	5 medium-sized shrimp (41/50 count)
Butter	paprika
2 slices Irish or Canadian bacon	splash of fresh lemon juice
4 spears asparagus, trimmed	chopped fresh parsley, for garnish
Salt and pepper	fresh fruit, for garnish

Prepare the Hollandaise Sauce, or, if you're using sauce that has been refrigerated, bring it to room temperature by warming it in a saucepan over very low heat.

Prepare 1 recipe Fingerlings (page 7), with or without Cajun spices, for serving.

Split and grill or toast the English muffin, then butter lightly. Fry the slices of bacon in a skillet over medium heat until lightly browned; drain on paper towels.

Blanch the asparagus spears in boiling salted water until they're just barely tender. Stop the cooking with a bath of ice water. Drain the asparagus well and sauté quickly in a hot skillet with a bit of butter. Season with salt and pepper and set aside.

Scramble or poach the eggs (see the box on page 46 for poaching method). Season the shrimp with salt, pepper, and paprika. Melt 1 tablespoon butter in small skillet over low heat, and sauté the shrimp until just barely opaque.

Toss with a little lemon juice, and remove pan from heat.

Place the toasted or grilled English muffin halves side by side on a plate. Place a slice of Canadian bacon on each, then top that with the eggs.

Arrange the asparagus spears between the English muffins and lay the shrimp in a row along the asparagus. Spoon the Hollandaise across the eggs, shrimp, and asparagus. Sprinkle with paprika and fresh parsley and serve with Fingerlings. Garnish the plate with fresh fruit.

Variation EGGS OSCAR NO. 2

This is more like the classic preparation of Steak Oscar. In place of the shrimp, use an ounce of quality cooked lump crabmeat on top of the eggs. In place of the Hollandaise, use Béarnaise sauce.

Eggs Galway

This recipe is another variant of Eggs Benedict, but with an Irish twist! Our brown bread is freshly baked in-house daily, and the recipe can be found in this cookbook. This is my very favorite breakfast, especially when I travel to Ireland! It is shown here with Home Fries (page 11).

1   Irish Brown Bread "Scone" (page 12), split in two horizontally

2   tablespoons vegetable shortening or butter

1   slice bacon

2   medium-sized eggs

2   tablespoons Hollandaise Sauce (page 28), or more if desired

2   thin slices smoked salmon or gravlax

Fried Capers (page 47), or plain capers, minced, for garnish (optional)

Butter the split sides of the Irish brown bread and toast or grill them. In a pan or the oven, fry or bake the bacon until crispy. Poach the eggs until set (see below). Place brown bread on a plate, grilled side up. Lay the bacon across both pieces of bread. Gently place a poached egg on top of each half of the brown bread. Top each one with a slice of the salmon and a spoonful of Hollandaise Sauce. Garnish with capers, if desired.

To poach eggs, bring 2 to 3 inches of water to a gentle boil in large saucepan or deep skillet. Adjust the heat to keep the liquid simmering gently. Break eggs, one at a time, into a custard cup or saucer. Holding the dish close to surface, slip the egg into the water. Cook eggs until the whites are completely set and yolks begin to thicken but are not hard, 3 to 5 minutes. Do not stir. Lift the eggs from the water with a slotted spoon. Drain in spoon or on paper towels. Trim any rough edges, if desired. Sprinkle with salt and pepper. Serve immediately.

Fried Capers

Capers are a delicious, salty, tangy, bacon-y addition to a plate. I've amped them up a bit with a quick fry, adding crunch and a nutty note. Fried capers are great on salads, in chicken dishes, or with seafood. They're also excellent as a topping for egg dishes that have Hollandaise sauce. They really are unique!

I credit Chef Mark Shadle from It's Only Natural in Middletown, Connecticut, and G-Zen in Branford, Connecticut, for sharing the idea. Toasted capers work well on salads or as a topping for egg dishes that have Hollandaise sauce.

Brined capers (whatever quantity you need)

Vegetable oil, for frying

Drain the capers well and blot between clean paper towels. Heat ½ inch of oil in a small to medium-sized pot (the size is dependent on the number or capers you're frying). When oil is hot enough for frying, add the drained capers. (When the oil starts to ripple, add a drop of water. If it jumps, then the oil is the right temperature.) Stir 3 to 4 minutes with a wooden spoon. Skim the capers out of the oil and drain on paper towels. Since the capers are brined in vinegar, they are not going to spoil. Store them in the refrigerator just like relish or pickles.

NOTE *The longer you leave them to dry on an absorbent paper plate or paper towel before frying, the better.*

Andouille Apple Crab Cakes

ANDOUILLE APPLE CRAB CAKES

Our original crab cakes were made with blue crabs. But every batch of crab cakes is unique, depending on the ingredients that are brought to us that day. Ingredients such as catfish, shad, and bluefish are often swapped out, depending on availability and freshness.

At one point, my Crab Cake Benedict special was a hit. While it was a big seller and had an amazing flavor combination, it reached a point where it became a staple. I eventually got bored with preparing the same dish every day, and decided to play around with the crab cake recipe to change it. This is one of my new favorites.

Using this recipe as a base, you can kick your dishes up a notch. I recently made a crab cake with crab, clam, and andouille sausage. Anything is possible. I use my martial arts strategy in my recipes—you can never be as good as you can be. You must keep pushing your recipes and taking them to the next level.

½ cup mayonnaise

½ cup prepared mustard

2 medium-sized eggs, lightly beaten

Heavy pinch of salt

Heavy pinch of black pepper

1 tablespoon Old Bay seasoning

2 tablespoons butter

½ cup finely diced andouille sausage

½ cup finely diced tart apple

¼ cup finely diced onion

¼ cup finely diced green bell pepper

¼ cup finely diced celery

2 pounds lump or claw crabmeat (2 [16-ounce] cans)

4 cups panko (bread crumbs)

Vegetable oil, for frying

2 tablespoons Hollanaise Sauce (page 28)

Fried Capers (page 47)

In a large mixing bowl, combine the mayonnaise, mustard, eggs, salt, pepper, and Old Bay Seasoning. Mix well and set aside.

Melt the butter in a medium sauté pan over medium heat. Add the andouille and sauté until it begins to brown. Add the diced apple, onion, green pepper, and celery and continue to cook until softened and lightly caramelized. Remove from heat and allow to cool.

Mix the sausage, apple, and vegetables into the previous mixture. Add the crabmeat and 2 cups of the bread crumbs. Mix well and allow the crab cake mixture to rest in the refrigerator for 30 minutes. This allows time for the bread crumbs to absorb the liquid.

Form the mixture into whatever size cakes you like, and coat with the remaining panko. Pan-fry the patties over medium heat until browned. Serve hot, with Hollandaise Sauce and Fried Capers.

Pancakes and French Toasts

Napoleon Pancakes

Napoleon Pancakes

The name Napoleon Pancakes is kind of an oxymoron, considering that Napoleon was short, and this stack is far from short!

We used to call pancakes griddlecakes, but today they are always done on the grill in our diner kitchen. At home you most likely will be using an oversize frying pan or electric frying pan.

Good pancakes call for good ingredients, and the key really is the mix that you use for your pancake. Aunt Jemima or any other name brand pancake mix will work. Great pancakes require the skillet temperature to be perfect as well as the viscosity of the batter. The skillet should be just above 350°F for the pancakes. The right temperature will create a pancake that browns around the edges and has bubbles in the middle of the batter before it's ready for flipping. If either temperature or batter viscosity is lacking, however, good old vitamin "L" (for love, of course) can certainly make up for it.

1 cup mascarpone cheese	2 tablespoons Peach Jam (page 56)
4 teaspoons honey	2 tablespoons Blueberry Jam (page 57)
½ teaspoon ground cinnamon	4 tablespoons Whipped Cream (page 58)
12 (4-inch) pancakes made from a mix or from scratch (see Note)	Confectioner's sugar, for garnish
	Ground cinnamon, for garnish
6 tablespoons Raspberry Jam (page 8)	Fresh fruit, for garnish

In a small bowl, mix the mascarpone, honey, and cinnamon together.

On each of four plates, spread 1 tablespoon of the raspberry jam. Place one pancake over the jam on each plate and spread with 2 tablespoons of the mascarpone mixture. Drizzle or spoon 1 tablespoon of one of the jams over the mascarpone. Repeat until all three pancakes are stacked with a layer of cheese mixture and jams in between each pancake. Top with whipped cream, and dust with confectioner's sugar. Sprinkle with cinnamon and serve with fresh fruit.

NOTE *At the diner, we use a good-quality commercial pancake mix because it gives us consistent results, and our customers rave about the pancakes.*

PEACH JAM

Making your own fresh jams and preserves at home is easier than you might think. Our products don't last long enough to spoil, but if you intend to keep yours for a long time, you can freeze or can them, using specific method for canning found online and in print.

I sometimes like to add Nice Spice (page 32) or a tablespoon of Peachtree Schnapps. The best time to make peach jam is in the summer, using fresh peaches. I make substitutions based on what is available at the time. At the end of summer, I will add a tablespoon of our house-made peach brandy to change the flavor a bit.

If you wish to make a peach-pepper jelly, simply add a jalapeño pepper.

4   cups peeled and diced peaches—either fresh or frozen is fine

¼   cup fresh lemon juice

6   cups sugar

1   (3-ounce) pouch liquid fruit pectin (I use Certo brand)

In a heavy-bottomed pan, bring the peaches and lemon juice to a boil over medium-high heat. Stir in the sugar and pectin, return to a boil, and continue to boil for about 1 minute. Transfer to glass containers and allow to cool. At the diner, we use so much fruit jam that there is no need for long-term storage. (At home you may want to follow proper procedures for canning or freezing jams.)

NOTE *Canning is a preserving process that can be carried out at home. I use Certo brand pectin; the instructions are excellent.*

BLUEBERRY JAM

For consistency, I use wild Maine blueberries. These berries are much smaller and are sweeter than the conventional berries. Around the Fourth of July, you will usually see me using blueberry jam on one of my French toast specials to make a "Red, White, and Blue" Bread Pudding. When making a cobbler, oftentimes I will replace some of the sugar in the cobbler recipe with blueberry jam, to add texture and fruit.

Once the basic recipe is mastered, you can make adjustments based on preference.

4 cups blueberries, fresh or frozen

1 tablespoon vanilla extract

7½ cups sugar

2 (3-ounce) pouches liquid fruit pectin (I use Certo brand)

2 apples, cored and quartered

2 pears, cored and quartered

In a heavy-bottomed saucepan, combine all the ingredients and gradually heat, starting on low heat, until they come to a simmer. Continue to simmer for 15 minutes, and then remove from heat. Transfer to containers and allow to cool. At the diner, because of the volume we use daily, we bottle our preserves in quart-size jars and refrigerate them. You could, however, can or freeze the jam, if you prefer.

WHIPPED CREAM

1	pint heavy cream
¼	cup confectioner's sugar
1	teaspoon vanilla extract

Whip all ingredients in a chilled bowl until stiff peaks form. Do not overwhip, or the whipped cream will turn into butter!

NOTE *You can substitute, but "whipping cream" is not as rich as the heavy cream I use at the diner.*

Variation FLAVORED WHIPPED CREAM

Substitute your favorite extract for the vanilla to create different flavor profiles—orange, rum, banana, crème de cacao, raspberry, and so on.

Banana Bread
French Toast

BANANA BREAD

The riper the banana, the deeper the flavor, so use the ripest bananas you can find. For an added decadent dimension, you can add white chocolate chips. (If you do, toss 1 cup of them in with the dry ingredients.)

You can vary this recipe further by substituting pumpkin, butternut squash, and so on, for the bananas, and by experimenting with the spice. At the diner, we use the Nice Spice blend. You can also choose to add your favorite spice—cinnamon, nutmeg, allspice, or whatever. If you are using this bread for French toast, refrigerate a day or so before making the French toast, for best results.

6	bananas, as ripe as possible
6	medium-sized eggs
4	cups all-purpose flour
2	cups sugar
2	cups vegetable oil
1	tablespoon baking soda
½	teaspoon salt
1	teaspoon Nice Spice (page 32)

Preheat the oven to 450°F. Grease 2 (9-by-5-inch) loaf pans.

Peel the bananas and mash them in a large mixing bowl. (You should have about 2 cups.) Add the eggs one at a time to the mashed bananas, mixing after each addition. Once combined, add the remaining ingredients. Mix until just incorporated—do not overmix! Pour the batter into the greased pans and place them in the oven. Reduce the heat to 350°F and bake for 15 minutes. Reduce the heat to 325°F and bake for an additional 15 minutes. Finally, reduce heat to 300°F and finish baking (about 15 minutes) or until an inserted toothpick comes out clean.

Banana Bread French Toast

Serves 4 to 6 (2 slices per person)

Featured on Diners, Drive-ins and Dives, *this French toast is a customer favorite.*

3 teaspoons butter

5 medium-sized eggs

½ cup sugar

2 cups half-and-half

1 teaspoon vanilla extract

1 loaf Banana Bread (page 60), made the day before and refrigerated

Bananas O'Rourke Topping (page 62), for serving

Whipped Cream (page 58), for serving

Preheat a griddle or large nonstick skillet over medium heat.

In medium bowl, whisk the eggs until well beaten, then add the sugar, half-and-half, and vanilla extract. Slice the banana bread into 1-inch-thick slices. Dip both sides of the banana bread into the egg batter. Place the battered banana bread slices in the hot, greased skillet and cook until both sides are golden brown, about 3 minutes.

Top with Bananas O'Rourke Topping and whipped cream. Add cookie pieces for a garnish if you like!

BANANAS O'ROURKE TOPPING

In 1951 the chef at Brennan's Restaurant in New Orleans came up with a solution for a surplus of ripe bananas. He made a sauce using butter, sugar, rum, and crème de banane and served it over ice cream. The original recipe from Brennan's was the inspiration for my version.

9	ripe bananas
1	cup (packed) brown sugar
1	stick butter
¼	cup Irish whiskey
¼	cup crème de banane liqueur

Peel and slice the bananas in half lengthwise, and then cut in half. Melt the butter and brown sugar in a large skillet over medium heat. Add the sliced bananas to the bubbling sugar. After 3 to 4 minutes, as bananas start to cook, add the whiskey and crème de banane. Be careful—if the butter and sugar mixture gets hot enough, it will ignite! Unlike in Bananas Foster, this version does not get flambéed, so remove the pan from the heat after adding the whiskey and crème de banane.

Pour over Banana Bread French Toast and serve immediately.

Variation **BANANAS O'ROURKE NO. 2**

Substitute 1 teaspoon vanilla or rum extract for crème de banane.

Irish Bread Pudding
French Toast

Irish Bread Pudding

At the diner we use the ends of sweet breads to make bread pudding. Each type of bread—poppy seed, pistachio, cherry vanilla, soda bread, almond pound cake, and so forth— creates a different flavor profile in the bread pudding. If using the pudding as a dessert, serve in small bowl with Lemon Curd (page 104), whipped cream, Raspberry Jam (page 8), Candied Nuts (page 67)— any sweet topping will do!

3 medium-sized eggs	1 teaspoon Nice Spice (page 32)
1½ cups half-and-half	5 cups cubed Irish Soda Bread (page 77)
½ cup sugar	Sweet dessert topping of your choice
1 teaspoon vanilla extract	

Preheat the oven to 350°F. Grease a 9-by-5-inch loaf pan.

Whisk together the eggs, half-and-half, sugar, vanilla, and Nice Spice in a large bowl. Evenly spread a third (a heaping 1½ cups) of the cubed bread in the pan. Pour a third of the wet mixture over the bread and let sit for 30 minutes, to allow the bread to absorb the liquid. Add another third of the cubed bread to the pan, and evenly spread it out. Pour another third of the wet mixture over the bread and let sit for additional 30 minutes. Evenly add the remaining cubed bread to the pan. Pour the remaining wet mixture over the bread and let sit for 30 minutes.

Create a water bath: Place the filled loaf pan in in a second, larger baking pan. Fill the larger pan with warm water until the water line is two-thirds up the sides of the loaf pan. Put both pans (one inside the other) in the oven. Bake for 1 hour and 15 minutes. If the pudding is not firm to the touch, lower the temperature to 325°F and bake for 15 minutes more. If the pudding is still not firm, lower the temperature to 300°F, bake another 15 minutes and check again. When the pudding is firm, remove the pan from the oven. Serve warm with a sweet topping of your choice.

Irish Bread Pudding French Toast

How do you make an Irish Bread Pudding even better? Turn it into French toast, of course! Top it with our house-made raspberry jam, and it takes this dish to the next level!

This recipe came from a cooking class I attended while in New Orleans. There, the concept was created to make use of excess dinner breads. At the diner, I actually use all the heels of our breads, and crumbs from cutting our sweet breads, to create unique bread pudding! This is a great way to use day-old cakes and turn them into something tasty. You could do the same by freezing your old bread.

Remember to place the Irish Bread Pudding in the refrigerator the night before making the French toast; when chilled, it's easier to cut.

Irish Bread Pudding (page 64), chilled overnight

8 medium-sized eggs

2 cups heavy cream

2 teaspoons vanilla extract

Large pinch of ground cinnamon

1 stick butter

Caramel Sauce (page 66), for serving

Candied Nuts (page 67), for serving

Cut the chilled bread pudding into 8 (¾-inch) slices.

In a mixing bowl, whisk together the eggs, cream, vanilla, and cinnamon. Pour into a pie plate or other shallow container and set aside.

Dip the bread pudding slices into the egg mixture and let them saturate for 30 seconds per side.

While the slices are soaking, add the butter to the hot griddle or pan and allow it to melt.

Cook each side of the bread pudding for 2 to 3 minutes, or until golden brown. If cooking in batches, put cooked French toast on a sheet pan, cover with tin foil, and keep warm in a 225°F oven while you finish cooking the rest of the battered slices.

Arrange two French toast slices on each of four plates. Drizzle a little Caramel Sauce over each to serve. A sprinkling of Candied Nuts makes a delightful addition.

CARAMEL SAUCE

I love this recipe, but I try not to make it too often because I'll end up eating it all. I love enhancing the flavor by adding vanilla extract to the sauce. Sometimes I'll use coffee as a substitute for the water.

1½   cups sugar

⅓   cup water

1   stick unsalted butter

½   teaspoon vanilla extract

1¼–1½ cups heavy cream

Combine the sugar and water in a heavy-bottomed saucepan. Heat on low until the sugar completely dissolves, stirring frequently. Increase the heat to medium and bring to a boil. Watch carefully; when the syrup reaches a medium-brown color, add the butter and vanilla extract and whisk until completely melted. Remove from the heat and whisk in the heavy cream. Cool to room temperature and serve, or refrigerate and warm the container in hot water for later use. The sauce will keep 1–2 days if refrigerated.

CANDIED NUTS

Candied nuts are very simple to make, and are a great garnish for several dishes. You can use any type of nut for this recipe, although cashews are my favorite. Beware, though: these are very dangerous to have in the kitchen. They are as addictive as they are good.

Butter, for greasing the pan

2 cups raw nuts of your choice

1 cup sugar

1 teaspoon vanilla

Grease a heavy sheet pan with butter.

Preheat a skillet over medium heat and add the nuts and sugar and vanilla. Reduce the temperature to low and wait for sugar to start to melt and bubble, about 5 minutes. Caramelization occurs once the sugar is bubbling slightly and the color has turned from blond to chestnut. Stir to coat. Remove nuts from pan and spread out on the greased sheet pan and allow to cool.

CIDER-POACHED PEARS

Without a doubt, fall is the best season for this recipe. My favorite pears to use are Bosc, Anjou, and Bartlett. Poached pears can be served as a side dish or used in a number of other dishes—poached pear with yogurt, poached pear with cereal, poached pear and pork sandwich.

To vary this recipe, substitute dried lavender buds, chopped (about ⅛ teaspoon for the vanilla and cinnamon to make a lavender-poached pear). Ginger paired with white wine works great as well! Once you have the basic recipe, you can work with different flavors to create new combinations.

2 (12-ounce) bottles hard cider

½ cup (packed) brown sugar

1 cinnamon stick

1 teaspoon vanilla extract

3 whole cloves

Pinch of nutmeg

6 firm ripe pears, halved and cored

Combine all the ingredients except for the pears in a large, heavy skillet over medium-high heat. Bring to a simmer, then add the pears and reduce the heat to low. Cover and cook on the lowest heat possible for 1 hour, turning the pears once. Remove the pears with a slotted spoon. Increase heat to medium-high and cook the liquid until it is thick and syrupy. Pour over pears. Serve cold or warm as a breakfast side dish or even over pancakes, or topped with Gorgonzola cheese and chopped walnuts as a dessert.

Whoopie Pie French Toast

MENU

Whoopie Pie French Toast with Assorted Toppings

WHOOPIE PIE FRENCH TOAST

This concept came from Sysco's former corporate chef James Brown. In a private food show, he created a menu for the diner that included an ingeniously transformed brioche bun: he took standard brioche, dipped it in egg custard, and then encrusted it in oats. I sometimes use a similar procedure with my Banana Bread French Toast and my Irish Soda Bread French Toast, as well as my Babka French Toast and our French toast specials!

2   medium-sized eggs

1   cup half-and-half

¼   cup sugar

3   teaspoons vanilla extract

⅓   cup old-fashioned rolled oats

1   tablespoon butter

4   Individual Babkas (page 72)

Ricotta Cheese (page 71), whipped cream (page 58), clotted cream, or other fillings and toppings of your choice

Whisk together the eggs, half-and-half, sugar, and vanilla in a medium bowl. Place the oats in a different medium bowl.

Melt the butter in a large skillet over medium heat. Split babkas horozontally, and dip them in the egg batter, then in oatmeal to form an oatmeal crust. Place the oat-encrusted babkas in the skillet and brown each side. Stack them with fresh Ricotta Cheese or jam in the middle, and top with anything and everything (shown here with fresh fruit and whipped cream)!

Ricotta Cheese

This fresh, soft cheese is easy to make and versatile. Mix with herbs or honey and spread on bread. Sweeten even more as a topping for pancakes or a cannoli filling. The separated whey can be used in a variety of baked goods and other preparations, should you be feeling thrifty. There are many recipes for making ricotta. The original was made from the whey left after making other cheeses— hence the name ricotta, which means "twice cooked."

I would like to thank Joe Mazzotta for teaching me how to prepare house-made ricotta. Joe is a concrete bricklayer who comes into the diner every Sunday. Several years ago, he brought ricotta in for me that he had made at home and told me how easy it was to prepare. The next week, Joe was in the kitchen teaching me how to make it myself. Today, it is a staple at the diner. It goes great with pesto, and I use it in omelets, as a topping, and as a key ingredient for many of our sweet breakfast specials.

½	gallon whole milk	¼	cup white vinegar
2	cups heavy cream	½	teaspoon kosher salt

Heat the milk and cream in a 6-quart stainless-steel saucepan slowly over very low heat. Monitor the temperature with a candy thermometer. Allow the mixture to slowly reach exactly 200°F. Stir in the vinegar and salt. Raise the heat to medium and watch until the solids of the cheese begin to form. This will be visible around the edges of the pan. Remove from heat and allow to cool for 15 minutes.

Strain the mixture by spooning it into a fine mesh strainer or colander that has been lined with a few layers of cheesecloth. Allow to drain for at least 30 minutes, or until the dripping stops. Reserve the whey for baked goods or other projects. (Whey could replace half the buttermilk in recipes using buttermilk.)

I received this recipe about twenty years ago from the mother of my good friend John Ziomek. This is a Polish bread that is known for being light and airy. I adapted the recipe, so that instead of making one large loaf, it makes individual, sconelike servings.

The key to success with this recipe is sifting the flour. Remember to make sure the temperature of the milk is reduced to 115°F after scalding before you add the yeast, or you will kill the yeast and your dough will not rise.

1	cup milk
1	stick butter, cubed, plus more for the cookie sheet
1	tablespoon active dry yeast
4	cups sifted all-purpose flour
2	medium-sized eggs
1	tablespoon sugar
1½	teaspoons salt
½	cup raisins
½	cup dried cranberries

Preheat the oven to 350°F. Grease a cookie sheet with butter.

In a saucepan, scald the milk over medium heat, then add the butter. When the butter has melted, pour the hot milk into a mixing bowl. Once the milk is lukewarm, add the yeast and remaining ingredients. After mixing the ingredients, knead the dough until well combined (5–10 minutes), or use a dough hook on a stand mixer. Divide the dough evenly into eight pieces and form into balls. Using the palm of your hand, press the dough pieces out to make mini discs about 1 inch thick.

Place on the greased cookie sheet and bake for 12 minutes. Lower the temperature to 325°F and bake for an additional 12 minutes or until puffed and browned.

*Irish Soda Bread
French Toast*

Irish Soda Bread French Toast

This recipe has been featured in both Yankee Magazine *and* Connecticut Magazine. *It is definitely a customer favorite, and it is ordered so often that I could probably make it in my sleep!*

1	loaf Irish Soda Bread (page 77)
6	medium-sized eggs
⅔	cup light cream or half-and-half
¼	cup sugar
1	teaspoon vanilla extract
¼	teaspoon salt
½	stick unsalted butter, or more as needed
	Strawberry Jam or Raspberry Jam (page 8), for serving
	Sabayon Sauce (page 76)

Cut the soda bread into 12 slices. In a large bowl, whisk together the eggs, cream, sugar, vanilla, and salt. Dip each slice into egg mixture, saturating well. In a large skillet, melt the butter over medium heat. Working in batches, place the slices in the skillet and cook until golden brown on both sides, about 4 minutes per side. Add more butter as needed. Keep cooked slices warm in an oven while you finish cooking the remainder of the French toast. Serve warm and top with Sabayon Sauce and jam.

SABAYON SAUCE

Also known as zabaglione sauce, this adds great flavor when poured over flan, bread pudding, or pancakes. For the liquor, you can add any flavor you desire. At the diner, I use Irish whiskey, but I also recommend Kahlúa or amaretto.

8   egg yolks, medium-sized

1   cup sugar

2½ ounces liquor of choice

Put the egg yolks and sugar in the top of a double boiler over simmering water. Using a whisk, beat the egg yolks and sugar together and continue beating as the yolks gently cook and thicken. When the mixture is thickened enough to fall in wide bands or "ribbons" from the spoon, add the liquor and continue to mix until thickened to the point where the top will stand in soft folds. Be sure to slide the double boiler on and off the heat during the mixing process to avoid cooking the eggs and creating scrambled eggs in your mixture. When it has thickened, remove from heat, cool, and pour into containers. (If you don't use the sauce right away, it can be refrigerated for 4 to 5 days. Before serving, you'll need to bring it back to lukewarm temperature by putting the jar in a hot water bath.)

NOTE *Sabayon Sauce is wonderful poured over raspberries or strawberries for a special dessert.*

Irish Soda Bread

There are lots of different kinds of Irish Soda Bread. This recipe for a rich, holiday-style bread is from an old Irish lady in Middletown. She always told me, "If you don't make it or bake it, sew it or grow it, you don't need it."

2½	cups all-purpose flour
1	cup plus 2 tablespoons sugar
¼	teaspoon salt
½	teaspoon baking soda
¼	teaspoon baking powder
1	cup golden raisins
2	medium-sized eggs
½	cup sour cream
⅓	cup vegetable oil
⅓	cup buttermilk
1½	teaspoons toasted caraway seeds (optional—see Note)

Preheat the oven to 350°F. Grease a 9-by-5-inch loaf pan.

In a medium bowl, whisk together the flour, sugar, salt, baking soda, baking powder, raisins, and caraway seeds (if desired). Form a well in the center. In a separate bowl, beat the eggs with a whisk, then beat in the sour cream, oil, and buttermilk. Add the wet ingredients to the dry ingredients, and stir with a wooden spoon or by hand until just combined (do not overmix). The batter will be thick.

Spoon the mixture into the greased pan and quickly put it into the oven. Bake until the bread is golden brown and a knife inserted into the center comes out clean, about 60 to 75 minutes. Remove from the oven, let the bread rest in the pan for 10 minutes, then invert on a wire rack and cool.

NOTE *Toast the caraway seeds in a skillet over medium-high heat for 2 to 3 minutes, or until fragrant, shaking the pan frequently.*

Variation SODA BREAD WITH IRISH WHISKY–SOAKED RAISINS

Soak raisins in Irish whiskey tea (page 31) overnight for added flavors. To make Irish whiskey tea, add 1 ounce of Irish whiskey to 2 cups of brewed Irish Breakfast tea.

Frittatas, Cheesecake, and Quiches

Harvest Frittata

I chose to make this recipe with a butternut squash crust because squash is a great fall vegetable. Many combinations can be used. Some of my favorite fillings are apple and Brie; pear, walnuts, and blue cheese; or prosciutto, spinach, and candied walnuts. This can also be made as individual portions in smaller baking dishes, as pictured.

FOR THE BUTTERNUT SQUASH CRUST

1   butternut squash (about 3 pounds)

¾   cup old-fashioned rolled oats

1   tablespoon maple syrup

½   cup chopped walnuts

     Pinch of salt

FOR THE CUSTARD

2½   cups heavy cream

5   medium-sized eggs

4   ounces Brie or other favorite cheese, cut into 1-inch cubes (if using Brie, leave rind on)

     Chopped herbs to taste (garlic, thyme, and rosemary)

Preheat the oven to 350°F.

A full-size butternut squash (approximately 10" long and about 3 pounds) will yield 2 cups of puree. Split the squash in half lengthwise. Brush with butter and salt. Bake covered at 350°F for approximately 1 hour, or until the flesh is soft enough to scoop out. Scoop the flesh into a 2-cup measure.

Make the butternut squash crust: Place all the ingredients for the crust in a large mixing bowl and mix together until thoroughly combined. Pat into the bottom of a 9-by-13-inch pan, just like a piecrust. Bake for 12 minutes; remove from the oven and allow to cool slightly while you are making the custard.

Make the custard: Place all the ingredients in a blender and combine until a custard is formed. Pour into the pan and place in the oven. Bake for 20 minutes, then lower the oven temperature to 325°F and bake until firm to touch, checking every 4 minutes.

Serve warm, cut into portions.

Red Flannel Hash

Red Flannel Hash is a traditional New England recipe. There are many stories about how it evolved. One is that can be traced back to Ethan Allen and Revolutionary days. Red Flannel Hash is corned beef hash with the addition of caramelized onions, bacon, and beets.

   At the diner, I love making this recipe the day after we've served a boiled dinner. It is a great way to enhance a traditional corned beef hash and turn your leftovers into a tasty new side dish. I like to top the hash with poached eggs to create a breakfast plate, but it can be used as a side dish for any meal—morning, noon, or night!

1   cup caramelized onions

6   slices bacon, cooked until crisp

2   cups mashed cooked potato

2   cups finely chopped cooked fresh or canned beets

4   cups hand-chopped cooked corned beef (about 1½ pounds)

1   medium-sized egg

¼   cup ketchup

¼   teaspoon celery seed

¼   teaspoon dry mustard

½   stick butter, for the pan

In a large bowl, hand-mix together all the ingredients, except the butter, until combined. Make into six patties, 3–4 inches in diameter. Melt the butter in a large cast-iron skillet over medium heat. Pan-fry each patty in the butter until both sides are golden brown, about 4 minutes total.

I first made this recipe in July of 1983. I adapted it from a recipe I found while vacationing on Nantucket Island. I now make these for the diner and also use them as part of my French toast specials.

3¼	cups all-purpose flour
1½	cups sugar
4	teaspoons baking powder
1	teaspoon salt
1	teaspoon Nice Spice (page 32)
5	medium-sized eggs
1	tablespoon vanilla extract
½	cup vegetable oil, plus a bit more to grease the muffin cups
⅓	cup walnuts, toasted
⅓	cup sweetened shredded coconut, toasted
1	(8-ounce) can crushed pineapple
1	apple, cored and grated
1	carrot, peeled and grated
⅓	cup golden raisins

Preheat the oven to 375°F. Grease 10 muffin-tin cups.

In a large bowl, whisk together the flour, sugar, baking powder, salt, and Nice Spice, then form a well in the center. In a medium bowl, beat the eggs well with a whisk, then beat in the vanilla and oil. Pour this mixture into the well of the dry ingredients and lightly combine. Fold in the remaining ingredients with a few quick turns. Scoop the batter into the greased muffin cups, filling them three-quarters full. Bake for 10 minutes at 375°F, then lower the temperature to 325°F and bake for 12 more minutes or until muffins are golden brown and a toothpick inserted in the middle comes out clean. They should sit about 15 minutes before you remove them from the pan.

NOTE *Muffins can be sliced when served, as shown in the photograph of this breakfast.*

Cheddar and Leek Frittata

CHEDDAR AND LEEK FRITTATA

Makes 1 (9-inch) pie

At the diner you will always find a frittata on our "Specials" menu. We make our frittatas in a 9-inch pie plate, but we also make individual frittatas in smaller vessels. For this frittata, I use just the white part of the leek, since that is sweeter than the greens.

1	cup sliced leeks, white part only
1	tablespoon butter, plus more for the pie plate
6	medium-sized eggs
3	cloves garlic, minced
1	teaspoon caraway seeds
1¼	cups heavy cream
½	cup shredded cheddar cheese
½	pound cooked sausage (optional)

NOTE *The upper green section of the leeks can be sliced thin and cooked until tender. (The green part will take longer to cook than the white.) Add to soups, eggs, and other savory dishes where you want some additional flavor.*

Preheat the oven to 350°F. Grease a 9-inch glass pie plate.

Trim off the leek roots and cut the leeks crosswise in two where the green and white parts meet. Slice the white parts lengthwise in half, and clean thoroughly under cold running water, then cut each half into thin lengthwise strips. Cut the strips crosswise into fine mince.

Melt the butter in a skillet and sweat the leeks for 15 to 20 minutes, covered, over low heat. (To "sweat" vegetables means to cook them slowly in a little bit of fat.) Do not brown! Remove from the heat and let cool briefly.

Beat the eggs in a mixing bowl, then add the rest of the ingredients, including the leeks. Pour the mixture into the pie plate. Bake for approximately 40 minutes, or until a knife inserted into the center comes out clean.

Serve immediately or warm, cut into wedges. (shown here with hand-cut fries and fried zucchini).

Risotto Cake

What is risotto? The name goes back to an Italian class of rice dishes that involves slowly cooking the rice in a broth to produce a creamy consistency. The main appeal of the short-grain rice is its ability to absorb liquid and to become stickier. Once cooked, it is blended with ingredients such as cheese or seafood and typically served as a first-course dish.

At the diner I tend to use risotto in an unconventional way. After making it, I chill it and cut it into shapes that I then dip in batter and fry. You can use, as I often do, a biscuit cutter to make a 3- or 4-inch round that can then be fried, baked or grilled, according to your preference. This recipe uses a standard pie pan.

1 quart vegetable stock or chicken stock (or salted water in a pinch)	½ cup white wine
1 medium shallot or ½ small onion, chopped (about ½ cup)	¼ cup grated Parmesan cheese
½ stick butter, plus additional for frying	1 tablespoon chopped fresh Italian parsley
1 tablespoon vegetable oil	Kosher salt and white pepper to taste
1½ cups Arborio rice	½–1 cup shredded mozzarella cheese
	Fried Capers (page 47)
	salsa

Bring the stock or water to a simmer in a saucepan. In a separate pot, sauté the onion or shallot in butter and oil over medium-low heat until just translucent. Add the rice and cook, stirring constantly, until you get a "nutty" smell—do not brown. Add the wine and cook, still stirring, for 2 minutes, until most of the alcohol has cooked off. Reduce the heat to low. Begin adding the stock or water a ladleful at a time, stirring constantly. Add more liquid, a ladle at a time, as soon as you see the previous addition begin to dry out, but before it's completely dry. The risotto is done when the grains are just cooked, but still al dente, in about 30 minutes.

Stir in the Parmesan and parsley, and season with salt and pepper. Spread the risotto in a greased 9-inch pie pan, and top with the mozzarella cheese. Bake at 350° for 10 minutes, or until the cheese is melted. Slice into wedges, and garnish with fried capers and your favorite salsa.

NOTE *Instead of using a pie pan, you can spread the risotto in a shallow baking dish lined with plastic wrap. Refrigerate until chilled and solidified. Cut the block of risotto into whatever shape you wish, or shape into balls or patties. Roll in breadcrumbs or cornmeal and pan-fry until golden brown on each side, about 3–4 minutes per side.*

Variation **MUSHROOM OR LEEK RISOTTO**

To make this an even more interesting dish, many other ingredients can be added to the cooked risotto: mushrooms, shredded carrots, leeks, and so on.

Savory Breakfast Cheesecake

Savory Breakfast Cheesecake

Makes 16 pieces

FRITTATAS, CHEESECAKE, AND QUICHES

Several years ago, I worked for a caterer and made countless sweet, fruit-filled cheesecakes. I mastered the traditional cheesecake recipe and was preparing the same dessert day after day. For those of you who have crossed paths with me, you know how difficult it is for me to stay within a set recipe without creatively altering it. As a result of my day in, day out sweet-cheesecake grind, I vowed to never make a sweet cheesecake again.

While vacationing, I found a savory ceviche cheesecake on offer at a nearby restaurant. I absolutely fell in love with the concept, and the thought remained in my mind until one day I decided to make my own savory cheesecakes. Today, you will find variations on savory cheesecakes on our "Specials" menu. This recipe is great as a breakfast or lunch dish, placed on a bed of salad greens or as a side dish.

Once the basic recipe is mastered, I encourage you to try different cheese blends and ingredients. One of my favorites is a combination of cream cheese and cheddar cheese. I also love to purée Brie and fresh herbs and add that mixture to the filling.

FOR THE OATMEAL CRUST

¾ cup old-fashioned rolled oats

¾ cup potato flakes

¾ cup bread crumbs

1–2 tablespoons melted butter

FOR THE FILLING

½ cup diced bacon

½ small onion, diced

1 clove garlic, minced

½ cup chopped turnip greens or mustard greens, leaves only

2 cups (16 ounces) cream cheese, softened

¼ cup grated Parmesan cheese

3 medium-sized eggs

Pinch of salt

Pinch of black pepper

Pinch of white pepper

Preheat the oven to 375°F.

Make the crust: Mix the crust ingredients together. Press into a 10-inch springform pan.

Make the filling: Cook the bacon until brown and crispy in a small skillet over medium heat. Add the onion and garlic and cook, stirring, until they begin to brown. Add the greens and cook until they begin to wilt.

In a mixer, with a paddle attachment, mix the cream cheese, Parmesan cheese, and eggs until smooth and free of lumps. Add the bacon-onion-garlic mixture, and mix until folded in. Add the salt, black pepper, and white pepper.

Spread the cream cheese mixture evenly over the oatmeal crust in the pan. Bake for 20 minutes, then reduce the temperature to 325°F and bake for another 20 minutes, or until the center is set and firm.

Allow the cheesecake to cool in the pan before cutting. Remove the springform sides, then slice the cheesecake and serve with Lemon Basil Aioli (page 92).

LEMON BASIL AIOLI

Aioli *gets its name from the Italian words for "garlic" and "oil." Aioli is great for sprucing up dishes visually, as well as adding taste. Infinite combinations are possible for this recipe. You can make an aioli of roasted red peppers, arugula, or anything else you may want to incorporate. It is great on sandwiches, omelets, egg dishes, fish, and chicken.*

1½   cups fresh basil leaves, cut into chiffonade (see Note, page 14)

1   cup fresh Italian parsley, stems removed, loosely packed

6   medium-sized egg yolks

4   cloves garlic, peeled

½   cup extra-virgin olive oil

Zest and juice of 1 lemon

Combine the basil leaves, parsley, egg yolks, and garlic in the bowl of a food processor, and puree. Add the olive oil in a slow, steady stream. Add the lemon zest and juice and blend until well combined.

The aioli can be kept covered in the refrigerator for up to 5 days.

Fried Green Tomatoes

In August and September, I use tomatillos. Right before the frost, I use green tomatoes. These are such a great addition to any dish and go well with gumbo. I like to use them as a sandwich topping as well.

2   cups all-purpose flour, divided

1   teaspoon Cajun seasoning

2   medium-sized eggs

1   cup milk

1   teaspoon salt

1   teaspoon ground black pepper

½   cup cornmeal

½   cup old-fashioned rolled oats

½   cup panko (bread crumbs)

5   tablespoons vegetable oil

8   green tomatoes, about the size
     of tennis balls, sliced

In a medium bowl, combine 1¼ cups of the flour and the Cajun seasoning. In another medium bowl, beat the eggs well with a whisk and then add the milk. In a large bowl, combine the salt, pepper, cornmeal, oats, panko, and remaining ¾ cup of flour.

Heat the oil in a large skillet over medium heat. Dip the sliced tomatoes in the flour mixture, then the egg mixture, then the cornmeal mixture. Fry the tomatoes until golden brown on both sides, about 6–8 minutes total.

Drain on paper towels and serve warm.

WINTER

Butternut Squash Quiche

Research shows the history of quiche going back to the German village of Lothringen. It became "Quiche Lorraine" after the French conquered Lothringen and renamed it Lorraine. Quiche Lorraine was filled with poitrine fumée, *or smoked breast meat. The original quiche did not have cheese and was made with strips of smoked bacon and custard.*

Once you are comfortable with this basic recipe, you can add different vegetables, depending on the season. If you like a creamier consistency, use heavy cream instead of half-and-half. At times, I like to make a crustless quiche—the variations are endless!

FOR THE CRUST

Option 1: Classic

1	cup vegetable shortening
2	cups all-purpose flour
1–2	tablespoons cold water

Option 2: Oatmeal

¾	cup old-fashioned rolled oats
¾	cup potato flakes
¾	cup bread crumbs
1–2	tablespoons melted butter

Option 3: Store-bought

1	package puff pastry sheets

FOR THE CUSTARD

1	cup roasted and mashed butternut squash (see method for roasting squash on page 82) or canned pumpkin or squash puree
1½	cups half-and-half
4	medium-sized eggs, beaten
½	cup shredded cheddar cheese
1	teaspoon chopped fresh herbs (parsley, sage, rosemary, thyme, or any you have on hand)

Make the crust: If making crust option no. 1, cut the shortening into the flour using a pastry blender or your fingertips. Add the water, and gently form the dough into a ball. Flatten to a disc, cover in plastic wrap, and refrigerate for 1 hour. Roll out with a floured rolling pin until the dough is about ⅛ inch thick (or 11 inches in diameter). Roll the dough onto the rolling pin, then unroll it over a 9-inch pie plate, gently pressing it into the pan.

If making crust option no. 2, mix the ingredients together in a bowl, then press the mixture into a 9-inch pie plate.

If making crust option no. 3, line a 9-inch pie plate with the puff pastry, cutting it as needed to fit the pan. Pie weights are not needed. Bake at 400°F for 15 minutes, or until golden brown. Cool before filling.

Make the custard: Preheat the oven to 375°F.

In a large bowl, combine all the custard ingredients, taking care not to overmix. Pour the filling into the pie plate and bake for 15 minutes. Reduce heat to 350°F and bake for an additional 15 minutes. Reduce heat to 325°F, and finish baking until set, about 15 more minutes. Let cool for at least 15–20 minutes before slicing.

ROASTED BEETS

Serves 6, as side dish

I like to get my beets directly from a local farm. The ideal size is a little smaller than a tennis ball. They are great sliced and served cold after roasting, turned into a red flannel hash, or as a sandwich topper.

Did you know that Swiss chard is from the beet family, as are sugar beets?!

12	beets, trimmed of leaves and stems
¼	cup olive oil
	A few pinches of salt and pepper

Preheat the oven to 350°F.

Peel the beets and place them in a roasting pan. Drizzle the oil over top of them and sprinkle on the salt and pepper. Cover with a lid or with aluminum foil. Bake for 30 minutes and then roll them over. Continue checking for doneness every 15 minutes. Beets usually take a total of 60 to 90 minutes to finish.

When beets are cool enough to handle, slice to serve.

APRICOT SQUARES

This recipe requires a little planning ahead, and few extra steps, but it's worth it. First, leave yourself 5 hours to soak the dried apricots before starting this recipe.

You will be making a shortbread and baking it, and then making an egg custard to pour over the top and bake a second time. If your squares come out too cakelike, add less flour the next time. You can substitute any fruit for the apricot. If you would like to add flavor to the shortbread, add some Nice Spice, fresh lavender buds, or your favorite spices! I also like to top the baked shortbread with a layer of chocolate chips, melt them in the oven, and spread them over the shortbread to create a chocolate layer in my apricot squares.

FOR THE APRICOT TOPPING

1 cup strong brewed Irish breakfast tea

3 tablespoons Irish whiskey

1¼ cups dried apricots

4 medium-sized eggs

2 cups (packed) brown sugar

1 tablespoon vanilla extract

⅔ cup all-purpose flour

1 teaspoon baking powder

½ teaspoon baking soda

FOR THE SHORTBREAD

2 cups all-purpose flour

½ cup sugar

1 stick butter, at room temperature

Soak the dried apricots: Combine the tea and whiskey in a bowl. Add the apricots and allow to soak for 4 to 5 hours (the apricots will expand, so choose a bowl with enough room).

Preheat the oven to 350°F.

Make the shortbread: In a medium bowl, combine the flour and sugar. Cut the butter into the mixture until a cornmeal-like texture is created. Press the mixture into the bottom of an ungreased 9-by-13-inch baking dish. Bake for 12 minutes, then remove from the oven and set aside. (Leave the oven on.)

Make the apricot topping: Drain the apricots and thinly slice them into small "match sticks," julienne-style.

In a large bowl, combine the apricots with remaining ingredients and mix together until incorporated. Pour over the shortbread in the baking dish, spreading the apricot mixture out evenly. Bake for 20 minutes, then reduce the heat to 325°F and bake for an additional 15 minutes. Reduce heat to 300°F and continue baking for 5 minutes or until the filling is set. (The filling resembles the filling in Fig Newtons.)

Cool for at least 15 minutes, then cut into 3-inch squares by scoring with a stiff square spatula. Cut and lift the squares out from the middle of the pan first.

SPRING

Asparagus and Brie Quiche

ASPARAGUS AND BRIE QUICHE *Makes 1 (9-inch) quiche*

Asparagus is fun to watch—it's one of the few vegetables you can actually see grow. Sometimes I use white asparagus, depending on the price.

1	recipe piecrust (option 1, 2, or 3— see page 95)

FOR THE CUSTARD

½	bunch asparagus, trimmed, steamed 1 minute, and diced
4	ounces Brie
1½	cups half-and-half
4	medium-sized eggs
	roasted asparagus spears, for garnish (optional)

Make the crust of your choice, remembering to prebake the puff pastry if you use it.

Preheat the oven to 375°F.

Make the custard: Put all the custard ingredients in a blender and pulse until they are incorporated. Do not overblend! Pour the filling into a 9-inch pie plate and bake for 15 minutes. Reduce the heat to 350°F and bake for an additional 15 minutes. Reduce the heat to 325°F and finish baking until set, about 15 more minutes.

Cool slightly before cutting into wedges to serve. Garnish with spears of roasted asparagus (if desired).

NOTE *Quiches can also be baked in individual baking dishes, as shown in the photograph.*

QUINOA SALAD

Quinoa is a protein plus. It is a seed from a grainlike plant that goes back thousands of years to the Andes of South America. I like to offer this with breakfast dishes in addition to lunch and dinner, because it is something I would eat. I like to snack on it throughout the day whenever I make it. This recipe can be served hot or cold, and seasonal fruits, vegetables, and herbs can be added to it for different flavors. It is a great base for chicken and fish dishes.

2   cups dried quinoa

2   tablespoons olive oil

3   cloves garlic, minced

1   medium onion, chopped

2   teaspoons lime juice

   Salt and pepper to taste

½   teaspoon chopped fresh sage, parsley, thyme, or rosemary

Prepare the quinoa according to the package instructions. Heat the olive oil in a 9-inch skillet over medium heat. Add the garlic and onion, and sauté until onions are translucent. In a mixing bowl, combine the sautéed garlic and onion (including olive oil from the pan) with the quinoa, lime juice, salt, pepper, and fresh herbs. Enjoy hot or cold.

NOTE *This salad can be served in a taco shell as pictured, if desired.*

Variation MANGO (OR TOMATO) QUINOA SALAD

Add minced mangoes and jalapeño peppers or add minced cucumbers and tomatoes, using only the meaty parts.

SPOTTED DOG

This is another type of Irish Soda Bread. I found a recipe online and made adjustments to create my own spin on the traditional recipe. This type of bread is a little less sweet than a traditional Irish soda bread, and it uses regular dark raisins (hence the spots) rather than golden raisins. These scones would be great with any topping—Raspberry Jam (page 8), Lemon Curd (page 104), Sabayon Sauce (page 76)!

4	cups all-purpose flour, plus more for the tops of the scones
2	tablespoons sugar
1	tablespoon baking soda
1	teaspoon salt
1	cup raisins
2¼	cups buttermilk

Preheat the oven to 350°F. Grease a cookie sheet.

In a large mixing bowl, sift together the flour, sugar, baking soda, and salt. Stir in the raisins. Create a well and add the buttermilk to the center. Using your hands, knead just until combined.

Use a large ice cream scoop (#20, which holds about 2 ounces) to place scone-size scoops of the batter on the greased cookie sheet. Sprinkle flour over each scone. Lightly press down to flatten. (If desired, these can be baked as muffins, as pictured.)

Bake for 12 minutes, then reduce the heat to 325°F and bake for 12 minutes more, or until browned on top.

Lemon Curd

This recipe reminds me of making ricotta because the temperature factor in both recipes is so important, and you can see the curds forming while you are heating them. Be sure when making this recipe that you do not leave the stove, or you will quickly see scrambled eggs in your curd. When zesting the lemons, you can use a vegetable peeler, just as long as you remove the white pith from the zest. When juicing the lemons, orange, and grapefruit, you can set aside any unused juice and add it to a jam recipe or use it for Hollandaise sauce. Lemon curd makes a great topping combined with raspberry jam for scones, cookies, shortbread, toast, crumpets, and more.

	Zest of 2 lemons
	Zest of 1 orange
	Zest of 1 grapefruit
1½	cups sugar
½	stick butter
4	medium-sized eggs
½	cup strained juice from lemons, orange, and grapefruit (¼ cup lemon juice and 2 tablespoons of each of the other two)
½	teaspoon Nice Spice (page 32)

Put the zest in a food processor with the sugar, and pulse until the zest is very tiny. Transfer to a mixing bowl and add the butter; stir together until combined. Add eggs, one at a time, stirring to combine after each addition. Add the strained juice and Nice Spice. Pour the mixture into a medium saucepan and set the pan over medium heat. Immediately begin stirring and continue stirring until the mixture thickens, about 10 minutes. **DO NOT LEAVE THE STOVE**

The mixture will thicken when it comes to 175°F on a candy thermometer (you can check, if you have one) and the eggs turn pale in color. You will also see curd starting to form. Remove from heat and pour into a clean heatproof glass container; allow to cool. Cover and store in refrigerator up to a week.

TOMATO BASIL QUICHE *Makes 1 (9-inch) quiche*

For this dish, I started with the basic quiche recipe and incorporated seasonal offerings to alter the flavor. This can be used as a main course but can also be served as a side dish when sliced thin. A variety of quiche can be found in my well-known "Brian's Breakfast," a breakfast sampler plate that changes daily according to what fresh ingredients are available. Part of the fun of ordering it is that customers never truly know what they will be served until their plates are set in front of them. The quiche is shown here with roasted potato slices.

1   recipe piecrust (options 1, 2, or 3—
     see page 95)

Make the crust of your choice, remembering to prebake the puff pastry, if that's what you're using.

CUSTARD

6   medium-sized eggs

½   cup diced onion

4   cloves garlic

6   fresh basil leaves, chopped (or 1 teaspoon
     dried basil)

4   plum tomatoes, peeled, seeded, and sliced
     (use only meaty parts)

2   cups half-and-half

¾   cup shredded cheddar cheese

Preheat the oven to 375°F.

Make the custard: With a whisk, beat the eggs in a large bowl, then incorporate the remaining custard ingredients, being careful not to overbeat or overmix. Pour the filling into a 9-inch pie plate and bake for 15 minutes. Reduce the heat to 350°F and bake for an additional 15 minutes. Reduce the heat to 325°F and finish baking until set, an additional 15 minutes.

Cool for at least 15 minutes before slicing and serving.

NOTE *Feel free to make this quiche in individual baking dishes.*

GAZPACHO

This recipe has Spanish origins, going back to the days of the Moors. It is very popular in the summer, and there are several ways you can serve and prepare gazpacho. Although usually thought of as a brunch item, gazpacho can be ordered at any time at the diner. Even if you go with the tomato base, you can vary it by using only diced tomato meat, rather than including the juices; however, gazpacho does not always require a tomato base! I also make twists to the basic recipe by substituting pineapple and coconut for the tomatoes. At times, I like to serve it in a martini glass with shrimp. One of my favorite gazpachos was prepared by my friend Jim Ladis, who is a martial arts master living in Chicago. Jim made his gazpacho with watermelon.

One thing I do not do is the bread thing! I do not like adding bread to the gazpacho, but rather serve it on the side. Instead, I suggest topping your gazpacho with Fried Capers (page 47). A basic gazpacho recipe is very similar to the pesto recipe, in that once you have mastered the basic recipe, the options for variations are endless!

10	ripe tomatoes, diced	2	tablespoons Worcestershire sauce
2	cucumbers, (peeled and) diced		Heavy splash of Tabasco sauce
1	red bell pepper, diced	2	tablespoons balsamic vinegar
1	green bell pepper, diced	2	tablespoons olive oil
1	medium onion, diced	1	tablespoon chopped fresh basil
4	cloves garlic, chopped	1	tablespoon fresh thyme leaves

Combine the vegetables in a large bowl. Peel cucumbers only if skin is thick or tough. Puree a quarter to a third of the mixture at a time in a blender, leaving some texture. In a second large bowl, combine the mixture as it is pureed with the remaining ingredients. Mix and serve chilled. Any leftover gazpacho can be covered and refrigerated for up to a week.

MENU

FALL Pumpkin
Brie Quiche

Baked Pears and
Candied Walnuts

This recipe is a version of the basic quiche recipe and is a great way to make use of your Halloween pumpkins. I like to use real pumpkin in my dishes when it's available; however, you can also substitute canned when pumpkin is not in season. In this recipe, roast the pumpkin. But you can steam or boil your pumpkin as well.

1   recipe piecrust (option 1, 2, or 3—see page 95)—remember to prebake the puff pastry, if that's what you're using.

CUSTARD

3   medium-sized eggs

1   cup roasted and mashed pumpkin (see Note) or canned pumpkin puree (about half a 15-ounce can)

3   ounces Brie, cut into small pieces, with rind

1   cup half-and-half

¾   cup shredded cheddar cheese

Preheat the oven to 375°F. Prepare crust.

Make the custard: In a large bowl, beat the eggs with a whisk. Then incorporate the remaining custard ingredients, being careful not to overbeat or overmix. Pour the filling into a 9-inch pie plate and bake for 15 minutes. Reduce the heat to 350°F and bake for an additional 15 minutes. Reduce the heat to 325°F, and finish baking until set, about 15 more minutes.

Allow quiche to cool for 15 minutes before cutting into wedges to serve (shown with a sweet bread and fresh fruit).

NOTE *If you want to use fresh pumpkin, here's how to roast it for puree (you can also steam or boil it). Preheat the oven to 350°F. Cut a small pumpkin (preferably a sugar pumpkin or cheese pumpkin) into pieces, then peel the pieces and cut into 1-inch cubes, removing seeds and stringy membranes. Place in a roasting pan and cover tightly with plastic wrap and then foil. Tuck the plastic wrap tightly under the foil, so that no plastic wrap edges are directly exposed to the heat. Roast for 1½ hours, or until very soft. Puree in a food processor or mash by hand until very smooth. Any unused puree can be frozen.*

BAKED PEARS AND CANDIED WALNUTS

This is an easy, tasty side dish for many breakfast entrées.

2 cups spinach, loosely packed

1 teaspoon olive oil

4 Cider-Poached Pear halves (page 68)

4 teaspoons crumbled blue cheese

2 teaspoons chopped Candied Nuts (made with walnuts; page 67)

Preheat the oven to 375°F.

Rinse the spinach in cold water and drain well. Heat the olive oil in a small saucepan. Add the drained spinach, and allow to cook for about 1 minute, until wilted, turning frequently. Remove the spinach from the pan.

Place the four pear halves in an 8-by-11 or 9-by-13-inch baking dish. Place a quarter of the wilted spinach in each pear cavity. Sprinkle 1 teaspoon of the crumbled blue cheese on top of the spinach in each pear half. Sprinkle ½ teaspoon of the chopped candied nuts on top of each half. Bake for 4 to 5 minutes, or until the cheese melts.

Serve hot or cold.

Other Breakfasts

Baked Stuffed Apples

BAKED STUFFED APPLES   *Makes 6 apples*

I have baked and stuffed apples many different ways. I suggest you choose a harder apple for this recipe, such as Granny Smith, Cortland, Baldwin, or Macoun. (I encourage you not to use Macintosh for this recipe. If you overbake a Macintosh, you will end up with applesauce.) Every apple is different, and once you find a type you like, stay with it. However, keep in mind that cooking times will vary depending on the type of apple.

6   apples

½ cup apple cider or apple juice

FILLING

1   cup Irish Granola (page 115)

½   cup raisins

   or

1½   cups shredded cheddar cheese

Preheat the oven to 350°F.

Use a pineapple punch (bigger than an apple corer) to cut out the core of each apple, but do not go through the bottom of the apple. You can also use a knife to circle the core out. Add the cider (or other liquid) to the bottom of a 9-by-13-inch pan, enough to coat the bottom and provide moisture, so that the apples steam. Cover with aluminum foil and bake for 20 minutes. While the apples are baking, mix together the granola and raisins, if you are using this as your stuffing.

When the apples are almost cooked, stuff them with raisin and granola mixture or cheddar cheese. Return to the oven and bake until the apple is soft and the cheese is melted, about 10 minutes.

Irish Granola

Granola is great for breakfast or as a snack. With the amount of nuts and fruit I add, this is my version of trail mix!

Using candied or toasted nuts adds extra flavor and texture to the granola.

6   cups old-fashioned rolled oats

½   cup honey

1   tablespoon Nice Spice (page 32)

¾   cup vegetable oil

3   cups dried fruits and nuts (raisins, dried cranberries, sliced dried apricots, nuts of your choice, chocolate chips, and so forth)

Preheat the oven to 350°F.

Put the oats in a large bowl and combine with the honey, Nice Spice, and vegetable oil. Spread the mixture out on rimmed baking sheets and place them in the oven. Bake until the granola is dry, crispy, and golden, approximately 35 minutes, stirring every 15 minutes. Mix in the dried fruit and nuts. When the granola has cooled, store in 1-quart containers or bags and enjoy with milk or yogurt, or just plain!

½ cup shredded coconut, sweetened or unsweetened

3 ounces cream cheese

1 cup sugar

3 medium-sized eggs

¾ cup sour cream

½ cup Candied Nuts (made with walnuts; page 67) or raw walnuts, chopped

½ cup crushed pineapple with juices (reserve about a quarter of the juices for glaze)

3 cups all-purpose flour

1 teaspoon Nice Spice (page 32)

1 teaspoon baking soda

½ teaspoon salt

FOR THE GLAZE

1 cup confectioner's sugar

½ teaspoon vanilla extract

1 tablespoon half-and-half

1 tablespoon butter, softened

Preheat the oven to 350°F. Grease a 12-cup muffin tin.

Toast the coconut: Heat a dry pan over medium heat. When hot, put the coconut in the pan and immediately remove the pan from the heat and toss the coconut, or it will burn. Keep tossing the coconut and, once it's brown, immediately remove from the pan and set aside.

Combine the flour, Nice Spice, baking soda, and salt in a bowl. With an electric mixer, beat the cream cheese and sugar in a second bowl until combined. Add the eggs, one at a time, continuing to beat. Add the remaining ingredients and mix until combined. Using an ice cream scoop (#20, which holds about 2 ounces), place scoops of batter in the greased muffin cups. Bake for 12 minutes, then reduce the heat to 325°F and bake for an additional 12 minutes, or until lightly browned on top. Cool in the pan for 15 minutes, while making the glaze.

Stir together the ingredients for the glaze, which should coat a spoon and "cry" (melt) when put on a hot muffin. If your glaze is too thin, add more confectioner's sugar. If your glaze is too thick, add more half-and-half. Pour the glaze over the warm muffins in the pan. Sprinkle the glazed muffins with the reserved pineapple juice, then remove them from the pan and serve.

Breakfast Shepherd's Pie

BREAKFAST SHEPHERD'S PIE

This dish, also called cottage pie, has been around since the 1800s. It is made up of a wide variety of ingredients. In the United States a traditional shepherd's pie consists of hamburger and peas; however, I sometimes use lamb, turnips, potatoes, and various toppings in my version. Broccoli and cheddar are some of my favorite additions, but I also like to prepare it with corned beef, bacon, onions, and eggs, as you will see in this recipe.

FOR THE CRUST

1 cup old-fashioned rolled oats

1 cup mashed potatoes

1½ tablespoons cold butter, cut into small bits

2 tablespoons grated Parmesan cheese

FOR THE FILLING

3 bacon slices

¼ cup diced onion

1 cup diced cooked corned beef

1 cup diced cooked potato (russets are good here)

5 medium-sized eggs

½ cup heavy cream

1 teaspoon chopped seasonal fresh herbs

A generous pinch of both salt and pepper to taste

Make the crust: Mix the ingredients for the crust together in a bowl until well blended, then press the mixture into a 9-inch pie plate.

Preheat the oven to 350°F.

Make the filling: Cook the bacon in a heavy skillet. When the bacon is cooked, remove and set aside. Sauté the diced onion in the bacon fat. Cook the onion for 5 minutes, or until translucent, then add the corned beef and diced potato and cook for 5 to 10 minutes, or until the corned beef and potato brown.

In a large bowl, whisk the eggs and add the heavy cream, herbs, salt, and pepper. Add the onions, corned beef, and potato to the egg mixture. Pour the mixture into the prepared pie plate. Bake for 20 minutes or until the egg sets.

ROASTED PARSNIPS AND APPLES

My definition of a parsnip is a pale carrot. The early Irish were known to use parsnip roots to make beer. In addition, history shows that parsnips may even be used in wine making.

1	pound parsnips
3	apples, cored, seeded, and sliced
2	tablespoons honey
½	teaspoon Cajun seasoning
2	tablespoons butter, melted
1	cup apple cider

Preheat the oven to 350°F.

Peel the parsnips and cut off the ends. Split any larger pieces in half lengthwise. Place the parsnips and apples in a 9-by-13-inch baking dish. In a small mixing bowl, combine the honey, Cajun seasoning, butter, and cider. Pour over the parsnips and apples and toss to coat. Roast uncovered for about 1 hour, then stir, and continue cooking until the mixture reaches the desired doneness.

HERB SCONES

Scones, donuts, cookies, muffins, and crumpets all have several similarities with biscuits. The history of a biscuit goes back to the fourteenth century, when the Dutch played with cookie recipes and eventually created the biscuit. My personal favorite biscuits are the thin wafers from England that are usually filled and spiced. In fact, a biscuit in England is more like a cookie than what we consider a "biscuit" in the United States.

But I love the soft, fluffy American-style biscuits that we serve at the diner, too. Vinny, our kitchen manager, has become our biscuit master and usually makes them by hand with either lard or vegetable shortening. We like to top our biscuits with sausage gravy, use them on Shepherd's Pie instead of mashed potatoes, add them to egg-based dishes, or substitute them for bread as a side for soups.

2	cups all-purpose flour
2	teaspoons baking powder
2	teaspoons salt
¼	teaspoon baking soda
1	tablespoon dried herbs (parsley, sage, rosemary, thyme)
7	tablespoons cold butter, cubed, or ⅓ cup plus 1½ tablespoons Crisco or lard, plus extra for greasing the cookie sheet
¾	cup buttermilk

Preheat the oven to 425°F. Grease a cookie sheet.

In a large bowl, combine the dry ingredients. Using a pastry blender or your fingertips, cut in the butter cubes until a grainy mixture is formed. Create a well and pour the buttermilk into the center of the bowl. Stir to work in the buttermilk until completely incorporated. Transfer the dough to a floured surface and knead lightly, but do not overwork. Roll out the dough with a rolling pin to a ½-inch thickness. Cut the biscuits to desired size. Place them ½ inch apart on the greased cookie sheet.

Bake for 12 to 14 minutes, or until golden.

Index

Page references in *italics* refer to photos.

Garnet Books

Titles with asterisks (*) are also in the Driftless Connecticut Series

Garnet Poems: An Anthology of Connecticut Poetry Since 1776* | Dennis Barone, editor

Food for the Dead: On the Trail of New England's Vampires | Michael E. Bell

The Case of the Piglet's Paternity: Trials from the New Haven Colony, 1639–1663* | Jon C. Blue

Early Connecticut Silver, 1700–1840 | Peter Bohan and Philip Hammerslough

The Connecticut River: A Photographic Journey through the Heart of New England | Al Braden

Tempest-Tossed: The Spirit of Isabella Beecher Hooker | Susan Campbell

Connecticut's Fife & Drum Tradition* | James Clark

Sunken Garden Poetry, 1992–2011 | Brad Davis, editor

Rare Light: J. Alden Weir in Windham, Connecticut, 1882–1919 | Anne E. Dawson, editor

The Old Leather Man: Historical Accounts of a Connecticut and New York Legend | Dan W. DeLuca, editor

Post Roads & Iron Horses: Transportation in Connecticut from Colonial Times to the Age of Steam* | Richard DeLuca

The Log Books: Connecticut's Slave Trade and Human Memory* | Anne Farrow

Dr. Mel's Connecticut Climate Book | Dr. Mel Goldstein

Hidden in Plain Sight: A Deep Traveler Explores Connecticut | David K. Leff

Maple Sugaring: Keeping It Real in New England | David K. Leff

Becoming Tom Thumb: Charles Stratton, P. T. Barnum, and the Dawn of American Celebrity* | Eric D. Lehman

Homegrown Terror: Benedict Arnold and the Burning of New London* | Eric D. Lehman

Westover School: Giving Girls a Place of Their Own | Laurie Lisle

Heroes for All Time: Connecticut's Civil War Soldiers Tell Their Stories* | Dione Longley and Buck Zaidel

Crowbar Governor: The Life and Times of Morgan Gardner Bulkeley* | Kevin Murphy

Fly Fishing in Connecticut: A Guide for Beginners | Kevin Murphy

Water for Hartford: The Story of the Hartford Water Works and the Metropolitan District Commission | Kevin Murphy

African American Connecticut Explored | Elizabeth J. Normen, editor

Henry Austin: In Every Variety of Architectural Style | James F. O'Gorman

Breakfast at O'Rourke's: New Cuisine from a Classic American Diner | Brian O'Rourke

Ella Grasso: Connecticut's Pioneering Governor* | Jon E. Purmont

The British Raid on Essex: The Forgotten Battle of the War of 1812* | Jerry Roberts

Making Freedom: The Extraordinary Life of Venture Smith | Chandler B. Saint and George Krimsky

Welcome to Wesleyan: Campus Buildings | Leslie Starr

Barns of Connecticut | Markham Starr

Gervase Wheeler: A British Architect in America, 1847–1860* | Renée Tribert and James F. O'Gorman

Connecticut in the American Civil War: Slavery, Sacrifice, and Survival | Matthew Warshauer

Inside Connecticut and the Civil War: One State's Struggles* | Matthew Warshauer, editor

Prudence Crandall's Legacy: The Fight for Equality in the 1830s, Dred Scott, *and* Brown v. Board of Education* | Donald E. Williams Jr.

Riverview Hospital for Children and Youth: A Culture of Promise* | Richard Wiseman

Stories in Stone: How Geology Influenced Connecticut History and Culture | Jelle Zeilinga de Boer

New Haven's Sentinels: The Art and Science of East Rock and West Rock* | Jelle Zeilinga de Boer and John Wareham